# THE NATURE OF

# REALITY . . .

Other titles by this author:

*Funny You Should Say That*, Seed Center, 1995
ISBN 0916108120

*Reality Is Just An Illusion*, Llewellyn Publications, 1999
ISBN 1567181554

*For more information, you may check www.chuckcoburn.com.*

10/10

Maxine —

Life has an interesting way of coming full circle!

Adym Coburn
www.thepsykic.com

# THE NATURE OF REALITY...

...and how to change it

Chuck Coburn

Copyright © 2009 by Chuck Coburn.

Library of Congress Control Number: 2009905847
ISBN: Hardcover 978-1-4415-4599-2
Softcover 978-1-4415-4598-5

All rights reserved. No part of this book may be reproduced or transmitted in any form or by any means, electronic or mechanical, including photocopying, recording, or by any information storage and retrieval system, without permission in writing from the copyright owner.

This book was printed in the United States of America.

To order additional copies of this book, contact:
Xlibris Corporation
1-888-795-4274
www.Xlibris.com
Orders@Xlibris.com
64277

# Chapter Summary

**Prologue** ................................................................. 11

**1—The beginning** ........................................... 15
On the seventh day, He rested * Creation stories * The evolution of life forms * Mankind's first appearance * What is the purpose of creation?

**2—Why are we here?** ...................................... 21
Nature of the universe * Who are we? * Created in His image * Ancient scriptures * The Dark Ages * Period of enlightenment * God's pattern

**3—A Few Clues** ............................................. 29
Numerous theories * Layers of existence * The nature of reality * A new way of thinking * Quantum physics * Power of positive thinking

**4—Levels of reality** ........................................ 35
The cosmic dance * Co-existence of time * What is consciousness? * Changing reality * Different points of view * Scientific support * Modify your reality

## 5—Reincarnation..................................................43
Ancient manuscripts * Power of the church * An argument for reincarnation * Redemption

## 6—Creating our own experience ......................48
Levels of consciousness * The Eastern view * Expanding consciousness * Dreaming * Understanding the symbols* Shaman dreaming * Living in the dreamtime * Gotta Believe * Community dreaming * The conception dream * The power of the dream

## 7—Co-creators with God ...................................61
The original sin * Falling from grace * Choices *Assistance from Ascended Masters * Trial and error

## 8—Taking Action for Change ............................66
A case in point * Misinterpretation * Discovering our higher purpose * Confronting karma

## 9—Predictions of the future...............................70
The Bible * The Oracle of Delphi * Nostradamus The Book of Revelation * Edger Cayce * The third secret of Fatima

## 10—The indigenous myths.................................77
The skeptics * Incan warnings * The legends of the Sioux Indians * The Hopi prophesies * Time capsules * How did they know?

**11—It must be working—we are still here** .................... 83
The gospel according to the National Enquirer * Can psychics read the future? * Moral implications

**12—Altering the Future**.................................................. 88
Does the future already exist? * Time is relative to the observer * New Age events * Cracks in time * Faster than the speed of light * Shaman physics *
Can healers change the future? *
The future is one of many possibilities *
Change the future

**13—Connecting with your Spirit Guides** ..................... 98
Unexpected messages * Recognizing the communication * Opening to the experience * Getting answers * Gaining confidence * Visualization

**14—Escaping With Our Lives** ...................................... 105
Indigenous living art * Running into trouble * Spirit guide intervention * An energy shift * A common connection

**15—Ancient tools—historical perspective** .................. 112
Fortune Tellers * Scientific proof * Psychic tools * Sacred energy * Charms & Amulets * Rituals & magic

**16—There are many paths** ............................................ 120
Why wait? * Going within * Six steps to non-attachment * Ten ways to higher consciousness * We are in the bonus round—want to really go out on a limb?

**17—The True Nature of Reality**.................................. 131
East vs. West * Taking it to the next level * Universal consensus * What is the lesson * Looking in the wrong place? * The bottom line

**18—Back to the Dream**.................................................. 138
The Creator's dream * Let go of your limitations * Expand your awareness * Dream the common dream * Access your higher knowing * Pay attention

*"'Come to the edge,' He said.
They said, 'We are afraid.'
'Come to the edge,' He said.
They came,
He pushed them . . . and they flew."*

*Guillaume Apollinaire*

# Prologue

This book is designed to provide a bit of insight into some of life's basic questions, such as the purpose of creation, who we really are and how we might attain spiritual consciousness. In short, it will examine the simple truth about reality... and how we can safely maneuver around in it.

One of the wisdoms derived from the New-Age mystics, sages and shamans is that we all have the capability to attain a higher state of awareness than we thought possible, not limited to just the centuries-old religious dogma of the dark ages nor the drug culture of the 60-s, but by forming a new thought process and understanding the *meta*-physics of what is. In order to do this, we must first discard some of the old paradigms that are no longer valid.

We need to learn how to think outside of the box... or at the very least, create windows in our box.

As you navigate through the chapters, you will learn about the evolution of matter and the development of individual consciousness from the beginning of time. We shall explore our personal relationship with the universe and the many levels of existence. We shall consider if there is a purposeful Creative Source, and if so, how and if we became separated from it.

Following a tour through a historical perspective of ancient belief systems, we will focus on a few who claim to have reached this Higher Consciousness, from Biblical prophets to modern-day soothsayers. We shall learn how different levels of perception can coexist simultaneously and how we can select and explore a personal reality that suits our life purpose. We will take a close look how "time works" and how some metaphysicians have claimed to be able to predict or alter the future. We shall conclude with a user-friendly crib sheet listing more than a dozen available methods one may pursue to attain higher awareness.

What is presented is a composite of ancient thinking and wisdom, salted with modern-day notions. This exploration of the purpose of creation will blend up-to-date scientific research and quantum physics with conventional spiritual dogma and New Age metaphysics, with a bit of the skeptic's point of view thrown in for good measure. We shall do all of this in order to understand that accessing this higher consciousness is possible from a variety of points of view, if only we follow a few of the clues presented herein and believe in the process.

It is the intention of this author to provide you with the tools to discover the structure of what is—the *meta*-physics of how things really work—in an easily read, non-technical summary of what is. I invite you to ponder what feels comfortable and sleep on that which feels foreign or awkward. After all, each has his own truths, each marching to the beat of a different drummer.

"But I learned all about life and how things are in school," you might say. You might point out that you paid attention during your educational process when your teacher discussed the rules of

## The Nature Of Reality...

Newtonian physics—you know, the gravity thing and why objects put in motion continue in motion until something messes with them. You might even be able to recall some of the old axioms in geometry such as "the shortest distance between two points is a straight line" and "all the traffic lights turn red when you are in a hurry."

Those rules have been updated!

So . . . if this prelude feels right then find yourself a comfortable space and prepare yourself for a journey. In the pages that follow you just might discover a few new guideposts on your unique path to increased awareness and spiritual freedom.

Hang on . . . here we go . . .

*Myths are clues to the spiritual potentialities of human life—Joseph Campbell*

# 1
## The beginning

Once upon a time, even before time began, "God created the Heaven and Earth. And the Earth was without form, and void: and darkness was upon the face of the deep. And the Spirit of God moved upon the face of the waters. And God said, 'Let there be light.'"

Then, after dividing the light from the darkness, He is said to have divided Earth from Heaven, and the land from the sea. The Bible goes on to inform us that by the fifth day, He had created "every living creature that moveth," right down to "every creeping thing that creepeth upon the earth."

Now, I don't want to spoil it for anyone who hasn't read the book but it was apparently well after He created the "creepy animal things," that He created man. An afterthought perhaps, or did He need to work out the kinks with the creepy crawly things first? Perhaps He saved his best creation for last, since it is written that we have been made in His image and given dominion over all things.

And on the seventh day He rested

Some have a problem interpreting these Biblical words literally. In spite of all the beautiful multicolored Sunday School textbooks we have read as children, are we to believe that this entire light, planet, mankind *thing* was completed in six 24-hour calendar days from start to finish?

Or did it just happen, you know, one atom bumping into another one and causing some sort of chain reaction that somehow eventually evolved into the rocks, trees and numerous highly complex life forms that inhabit this tiny little spot in our immense universe.

Perhaps we are to accept our scientific community's hypothesis that the creation process evolved out of some inexplicable glob of energy that somehow happened to be there. Cutting through the technical hyperbole, we are taught that matter and form appeared and evolved as a result of a variety of chemical reactions and natural evolution, in six or more "ages," or time periods.

Was this the masterstroke of a sudden flash of inspiration by a purposeful deity or, as some might believe, a more laborious and erratic development punctuated and tempered by numerous arbitrary and spontaneous events that simply occurred randomly?

Creation stories

There are as many variations of the planetary creation stories that have been handed down from generation to generation, as there are cultures on this planet. The Bible, of course, states that it is the net result of "the Word of God." The original inhabitants of the American Southwest, on the other hand, believed that Spider Woman created the physical world from her location high atop a narrow column of rock. The legions of the Australian aborigines from Arnham Land suggest that it wasn't either a single event or one powerful energy field, but a committee of ancient ancestral spiritual beings that created the landscape, mountains and waterways during "the dreamtime."

Was this the work of independent spiritual designers or the thought of a single, Creator Force?

Joseph Campbell, who spent most of his life studying ancient societies, suggested that all myths and legends are stories that have a root in truth, spun in a form that characterizes the people they represent. Although the many legends vary, there appears to be a common thread suggesting some conscious force gave physical existence its initial inauguration. After all, how can something as immaterial as consciousness ever arise from something as unconscious as matter?

Of course there are those who question the existence of any sort of Master Force with or without a specific agenda or master plan. These same folks might suggest that all of this just happened—like a big lab accident.

However, when asked who built and furnished the lab they are strangely quiet.

## The evolution of life forms

Taking this avenue of exploration to the next step, let's look at the issue of the advent of mankind. Did humankind literally take its initial breath in the Garden of Eden in one magical, mystical and glorious grand moment? Or did our pre-ancestors evolve from wiggly—squiggly things that crawled out of the mud over time and then swing from trees for awhile before evolving into our present form and dividing themselves into groups such as Asians and Africans, carnivores and vegetarians, Republicans and Democrats?

Russell Vreeland and William Rosenzweig of West Chester University in Pennsylvania believe that life forms on our planet initially evolved from spores of living organisms that were somehow transported from planet to planet, across the galaxy and over eons. These scientists drilling into a New Mexico rock formation deep underground have brought to life unknown strains of bacteria that have lain entombed in salt crystals for over 250 million years, giving credence to a concept they call "panspermia" to explain the original source for life on Earth. [1]

Birger Rasmussen, a geologist at the University of Western Australia and Stefan Bengtson, a paleontologist at the Swedish Museum of Natural History have discovered what they have determined to be evidence of life forms that even predate Vreeland and Rosenzweig's find. They made several discoveries including what appear to be "the tracks of tiny wormlike creatures that oozed their slimy way across the mud of a tide-swept seashore at least 1.2 billion years ago." [2]

## Mankind's first appearance

Most scientists agree that the big bang occurred about 13.7 billion years or so ago, give or take a millennium, and that all forms of life that swim, crawl, walk, run or fly emerged over millions of years. This, of course, is in direct conflict with a few religious scholars who might have us believe that the origin of our species is much more current with mankind making its first appearance in Samaria around 5,000 to 6,000 years ago.

If this latter argument is true, how do we explain the cave drawings carbon dated over 30,000 years ago or humanoid skulls thought to be millions of years old?

Some have even suggested that human existence might have actually begun millions of years earlier than previously believed and was destroyed and forced to reinvent itself. There is recent evidence to suggest that the Earth's poles may have shifted at least once and that the Sahara desert was once a polar cap and that the North Pole supported warm-blooded animals at one time. Perhaps this cataclysmic event wiped out an earlier civilization or two, lending credibility to the popular Atlantis and Lemuria stories first recorded by Plato.

A few researches, with somewhat less impressive credentials, take a somewhat different tack, claiming that we are actually the direct descendants of space travelers, forced to leave a dying planet. Others of a like mind have suggested that we are the products of an advance team from a seed community located in a distant galaxy whose mission was to spread intelligent life throughout the galaxy.

Whatever we might choose to believe, it is hard to imagine that it all just happened by chance.

## What is the purpose of creation?

If we are to believe in a Creative Spirit, there is the ultimate question—why? What was Its motivation and purpose for creation?

If from all this we can conclude that there is a God-like force, were we humans created for a specific purpose or are we merely a collective cosmic joke intended to entertain the gods? Are we separate souls who are somehow being tested, risking eternal damnation should we fail to follow the strict laws handed down by a religious few wearing fancy robes and special pointy hats? Or, instead, since we are said to have been created in His image, are we free spiritual extensions of this Powerful Force, reincarnating time and time again in order to seek a true understanding of what exactly is, is?

If reincarnation does in fact take place providing us numerous opportunities to experience life in a physical form, where do we go between lifetimes when the soul or life force leaves the physical body? Up? North by Northwest? Is there journey after death, as is illustrated in the hieroglyphics and paintings on the walls of the ancient Egyptian tombs? Do the ancient texts of the Sumerians suggest insight? Or do we all hang out in some kind of deep slumber, awaiting the "judgment" of some condemnatory Deity following the "last days" or "Second Coming?"

Let's explore some of the possibilities . . .

> *We shall not cease from exploration—And the end of all our exploring—will be to arrive where we started—and know the place for the first time.—T.S. Eliot*

# 2

# Why are we here?

Descartes, a heady 17th century philosopher began his search for some of these same answers by beginning with the basic question, "Do I exist at all?" We are told that after many years of struggling with this quandary he finally determined that he did by penning the immortal words, "I think, therefore I am." Most of us would probably agree with his conclusion, if for no other reason than if you got this far into this book, something must be going on.

So now let's get to a tougher question such as why do we even exist? And further, are we individual and separate cosmic beings or individual reflections of a singular Godhead, if indeed some sort of purposeful Creative Energy even exists at all?

## Nature of the Universe

If we were to examine the nature of the universe—from the precise balance within the numerous vast galaxies to the makeup of a simple atom, we would discover that *everything* appears to be an integrated portion of a larger whole. Therefore, to suggest that we are separate beings without direction or inner dependence would appear to go against the pattern of everything that occurs in nature. In light of just this single observation, to conclude that we are nothing more than the net result of a random, purposeless existence that just somehow happened to come about out of the void of nothingness might seem to defy simple logic. We might then conclude that if this were true, "something" probably had to design and create the complexities of what we know as consciousness and physical existence.

Creation suggests that everything appears to be a part of a larger whole, and there also appears to be continuity in nature. Spring turns to Summer and Fall and dies off in the Winter, only to be reborn the next Spring. Rain falls from the sky, supports life and is eventually discarded, only to be reabsorbed into the sky to fall once more as rain.

## Who are we?

Having some assurance now that we do in fact exist, and that there seems to be some larger intelligent order to things, we might next wish to ask what exactly is our purpose? But to understand who we are, first we might wish to define what this larger whole or Creative Energy is, and why It provided us life and form.

Let's go back to the Bible where it is written that God said, "Let us make man in *our* image, after *our* likeness . . ." Does this statement raise more questions than it answers? If we are made in God's image does that mean that we look just like Him or Her? Is He or She tall or short, male or female, black, yellow, red or white? And what is meant by "our" in the above quotation? Doesn't the use of the word "our" imply more than one entity? Does this suggest that He or She is some sort of Collective Committee or Thought rather than a single image?

# The Nature Of Reality...

Everyone who paid attention in Sunday School can tell you what God looks like. Pick up any illustrated religious text written for children and you will see that God is a white-skinned male, a single entity, probably about 90 years old, six feet tall, sporting a white beard and dressed in an old fashioned, heavy-looking robe. If that is not enough, Michelangelo provided a clear visual for us on the ceiling of the Sistine Chapel. Are we really intended to take this corporeal description as a literal true and accurate representation of the Deity's physical appearance?

It is said that because He (let's use the masculine pronoun for convenience) was the original creator, He has always been, existing even before time was; therefore, since He created all physical form, He had to be "there" *before* there and form even existed.

If that were true, could we not conclude that He is above physical form—Energy vibrating at an extremely high rate?

## Created in His likeness

We might ask how we could be created in His form if He is without a body and, therefore, without physical form? Might this suggest that if we are created by, or we are extensions of God, we are primarily units of energy? Does it follow, then, that our physical bodies are merely an extension of our energy bodies manifested into a physical environment? Is that which looks back at us in the mirror simply a reflection of the spiritual essence of who we are?

I feel confident that most Biblical scholars would probably concur that God is more likely a spiritual force rather than a physical figure. After all, Moses was an eye-witness and described Him as pure energy—a strong light or burning bush—not a man or woman. The Bible refers to Him as, "I Am That I Am," suggesting some sort of totality of all things. The fact that it claims that we are made in his image would suggest we all are an extension of that Allness.

If we have been made in His image, and if it is said that He has always been and will be forever, then we must be not only individual expressions of this universal energy, but eternal expressions of it as well. Perhaps in the beginning there existed a sea of consciousness or spirit that began to awaken. Being a single thought, it had no way of knowing what it was without something to reflect Its image—kind of an Adam and Eve thing. Perhaps it divided itself in a second thought, much as a single cell does, following the moment of conception.

Becoming restless and wishing to discover Itself, It may have imagined Its' vibration into individual portions that eventually became the life essence or building blocks of the Universe; grains of sand, as it were, as part of a cosmic beach.

As this Universal Mind further expanded on Itself, individual consciousness formed and slowly became aware of its separation and existence apart from the Primary Source. Had it not done so, it would have remained an undivided part of the Whole.

Since everything in nature has its season, one might conclude that each individual consciousness will not be terminated but will eventually return to its Origin once it becomes fully realized and in harmony with the Source. Since the Creator would have little reason to destroy an extension of Itself, each individual part would again become a part of the Whole while realizing its individual existence as a part of the larger Essence it gained while in physical form.

## Ancient scriptures

The Vedas, the 4,500 year-old ancient scriptures of the Hindu religion support this thought: God, or Brahman, is a supreme spirit and each person's spirit, or Atman, is the expression, extension or manifestation of this One Absolute Infinite Being.

Lao-tse, the founder of the Taoist religion in China over 500 years before the birth of Christ, saw God as a great spiritual power that controls the universe. His teachings postulated that Heaven, earth and man were all components of this Great Spirit, created to act in divine harmony with each other.

The Qabbalah, the "secret doctrine" of Israel, professes the same truth. It is believed by some that God instructed Moses on its principles on his third trip up Mount Sinai. Moses recorded the secret teachings in the first four books of the Pentateuch. Early initiates of the Qabbalistic Mysteries believed these truths were originally taught to the angels by the word of God before the fall of man. Its basic doctrine states that all life is one in essence and that man is a miniature replication of God or the Great Universe. [3]

Others professed similar thoughts, such as Zoroaster, a Persian prophet who founded Zoroastrianism, Buddha, Confucius and, of course, Jesus. Each taught in his own way not only that man was an aspect of God but also that non-perfections such as sickness and limitation were illusions.

## The Dark Ages

Of course, this concept that we are an extension of the Creator Force has not always been the dominant thought. From about 500 AD to 1500 AD the world went through the Dark Ages, and this understanding became muddled during this era of turbulence, invasions and warfare. Religious thinkers began to view the Divinity differently.

In the seventh century, Mohammed, the founder of the Islamic religion began teaching that peace could only be attained by complete and total *submission* to the powerful will of God.

At the same time, the Catholic Church, the major spiritual force in Europe, taught that man was separate from God and that the Church was the only true means to a positive afterlife. Fear and guilt were introduced, suggesting that we were to fear God and that the devil would "get us" if we were not devoted to the specific interpretation of scripture by the church

In the eighth century, the armies of this Church of Rome attempted to reclaim the "Holy Lands" from the Muslims regardless of who got in their way. This was followed by the infamous Crusades that began in 1095 and, in one form or another, continued for the next six hundred years.

In 1212 an event known as the Children's Crusade resulted in the deaths or enslavement of thousands of children. In 1231, Pope Gregory IX sent his teammates through much of Europe, destroying entire cultures that did not believe in his particular brand of truth. In 1252, the Pope, ironically named Innocent IV, imprisoned and tortured many of those whose beliefs did not correspond with his. In 1498 Pope Sixtus IV appointed a delightful chap named Tomas de Torquemada to be the Grand Inquisitor. Torquemada eventually burned well over 2,000 alleged heretics to their slow and painful deaths. Even Galileo was tried by this religious based judicial system and condemned to house arrest just because his point of view regarding the movement of the planets was contrary to Holy Scripture. [4]

## Period of Enlightenment

Then, in the sixteenth century following the advent of the Protestant Reformation, Lutheranism, Calvinism, Anglicanism and most of the subsequent splinter groups that followed began to modify this strict concept of man's separation from God. A few philosophies, such as the Rosicrucians [5] and Hermeticists [6] suggested that the universe is basically a mental realm rather than a physical one. They believed that everything exists purely as a thought in the Mind of God, or the All That Is. As Steven Pressfield elaborates in his book, *The Legend of Bagger Vance* [7], "we human beings with all our complexities had no substantial existence as matter, but were merely thoughts in the mind of our Creator, much like Micaber [8] arising with his fellows from the mind of Dickens.

In the 1800's, a new movement called Transcendentalism reinforced this new thought, philosophizing that the soul can transcend the senses and achieve a direct relationship with God. Transcendentalists believed that all people are able to commune directly with the Supreme Creator. They postulated that each of us possesses the ability to intuitively grasp the ultimate truth on our own. They contended that the churches did nothing but institutionalize God by viewing him as a powerful distant and indifferent force in order to retain their sway over the masses.

As John Randolph Price points out in his book, *The Planetary Commission* [9] Ralph Waldo Emerson, became a principal spokesman for this new transcendental movement. He wrote, "From within or from behind, a light shines through us upon things and makes us aware that we are nothing, but the light is all." Referring to Jesus he said, "He saw that God incarnates himself in man, and evermore goes forth anew to take possession of his world." Later he added, "We are what we think about all day long."

This new thinking paved the way for Phineus Quimby (1802-1866), a metaphysician who provided the early foundation of Mary Baker Eddy's Christian Science. Additional churches sprang up with a variation of this theme such as Divine Science, Religious Science and Unity Church, all teaching the inseparable oneness of God and man.

## God's pattern

Whether you label this as God's intervention, His master plan or Light Bearers or Angels of Light descending on the planet, there seems to be a pattern here. Many would contend that this was the same awareness that originally awakened the consciousness of early man which had become trapped in animal consciousness. They would tell you that it was the same light that guided the building of early temples. The periodic disappearance or misuse of this light is reflected in the fall of man as described the Bible: the destruction of Atlantis, the Great Flood and the Dark Ages, to mention a few examples.

Whatever you consider Him to be, either He has incredible patience to continuously reinstate the light after we have attempted for centuries to snuff out the flame of enlightenment, or time has little meaning and life is really just a pointless, endless moment of now.

Either we are caught in some sort of time loop like Bill Murray in the movie *Ground Hog's Day* . . . or we keep coming back time and time again . . .

. . . until we get it right.

> *The best and most beautiful things in the world cannot be seen or even touched. They must be felt with the heart.* —Helen Keller

# 3

# A Few Clues

As we have seen, we might garner some inkling of understanding about who we are and our connection to a Master Creator in the sacred texts of a few of the major religions. In addition, ancient traditions, oral stories and ceremonies kept alive in remote, indigenous cultures may offer some additional perspective. Even the indecipherable symbols scrawled on ancient monolithic structures constructed by mysterious civilizations offer clues and provide some understanding.

## Numerous theories

Many theories, of course, are postulated from a large body of thought—from the left brained, dedicated men and women investigating the mysteries of science to the right-brained, self-professed spiritual gurus channeling what they perceive as spiritual truth. Mix all of that with a splash of pure speculation emanating from New Agers proudly displaying a variety of jewelry hanging from holes drilled in their faces, and you are provided a wide range of possibilities from which to choose.

There are, naturally, no easily defined answers to these quandaries and mysteries. But even if there were, to some skeptics no amount of proof would be enough. As a professional psychic for over 30 years, I have spent time with many indigenous tribes and witnessed bizarre healings. I have spoken with and redirected deceased spirits as well as located missing objects and runaway children. I have channeled numerous individual psychic readings and must have been accurate based on my long waiting list for a session. Yet with all of that, a group of self-proclaimed open minded people in Northern California who call themselves the *Bay Area Skeptics* and have offered $10,000 to the *first* person who can *prove* a psychic event, still have their money in the bank.

Perhaps the fact that we each need to personally search for our own personal truth is part of the adventure.

It may be no accident that some of this information has purposely been kept hidden from us by self proclaimed secret societies in order that they might retain their power. Perhaps the Universe in its eternal wisdom has required each of us to conduct our own personal search in order that we might come to discover that life is not limited to a precise, single level, ego based, means of consciousness and existence. In order to better understand this statement, let's examine that which is readily at hand—physical existence—the familiar world in which we function on a day to day basis.

## Layers of existence

I think we would all agree that our outer world, or at least our conscious awareness of our physical environment, exists on a multitude of layers and functions within well-defined and predictable physical laws. The earth revolves around the sun, day follows night, and spring follows winter. We are able to predict how physical matter will act and react within predetermined mathematical certainties by applying specific well known laws of physics. For example, an object set in motion shall remain in motion unless interrupted by an outside force. Basically rocks remain rocks unless altered by an extraneous element, such as heat, water, wind, and so on. We know that when we go to sleep at night our toothbrush will be right where we left it and the color will not have changed unless someone has messed with it.

For many, life is like that: strictly defined and limited by what they see and expect. These same people might theorize that life has one basic pattern: we are born, we live and then we die. They might contend that life is nothing more than individual random moments of existence, with little or no meaning.

This point of view suggests that life is extremely arbitrary, with some people capriciously relegated to a life of suffering and poverty while others are somehow lucky enough to be born into a wealthy family and enjoy a life of leisure until death eventually overtakes the body and individual existence ends.

## The nature of reality

These are often the same people who feel they are unlucky and blame a variety of outside forces that prevent them from getting what they want. They are the ones who always seem to pick the wrong line at the bank or become resigned to the fact that the last parking place will be claimed by the guy in front of them. They see their lives as the product of circumstances beyond their ability to influence the outcome. Basically their philosophy might be summed up to be something like, "what you see is what you get."

But is it? Is there but one level to life and living? Is only what you see touch and feel the entire extent of your universe?

The cave man thought so. He took in stride what life dealt him. He thought all of existence was what he could see in his line of sight. It took someone with a daring sense of adventure to wander over the mountain to see that there was another side.

The more educated man of the Middle Ages thought so, too. He believed that the world was flat and that he was at the center of the universe. It took daring explorers such as Lief Erickson, Christopher Columbus and others to convince all of Europe that we would not fall off the edge. It took far-reaching thinkers such as Galileo and Copernicus to propose the novel idea that the earth was only a small, insignificant ball almost lost in the entire universal scheme of things.

## A new way of thinking

Now we have new postulates or theories about the nature of reality and its interconnectedness. No longer do modern thinkers believe we are autonomous beings acting independently from one another. Look at most societies: people seem to huddle together in big cities. People require the approval of others and have the need to be liked, accepted in order to fit it. Sure, there are those who may profess to go it alone and take pride in the fact that they march only to their own drummer, but are they not adapting to a group dynamic requiring them to display their collective separateness as well?

Seldom in nature do we observe things standing alone. Planets in the solar system revolve around each other. Most species depend on others of their kind for reproduction and survival.

## Quantum physics

This idea was taken to the next level in the mid-1940s when many of the two dimensional rules of science were forever changed with the advent of the splitting of the atom and the birth of quantum physics. Where old-fashioned Newtonian physics suggested each event in nature stood alone, Quantum physics postulates that no particle is really independent from all the rest.

Russel Targ, renowned physicist and author as well as prominent Stanford University research scientist reports that laboratories have proved that particles once thought to be independent of each other are somehow intertwined in the larger scheme of things. By using extremely advanced instruments that can measure such things, scientists have demonstrated that light beams emitted in opposite directions from a source traveling at the speed of light actually maintain their connection to one another. It is as if they have a higher sense of the sum of all their parts. Each photon is somehow affected by what happens to its twin, many miles away.

We don't need to turn our attention away from our own bodies to find another prime example of this concept. Medical researchers have long marveled at the apparent interconnectedness of the many stem and nerve centers of our bodies as if they are all connected to the larger body mainframe computer. Athletes will tell you that in order for a team to be competitive, each player has to become an extension of the whole, almost as if they knew what the others will do, as if tuned into a common consciousness.

Are we conscious of our source and interconnected with others around us? If you think otherwise, how do we explain mothers who seem to know when a family member is in danger? If you doubt this is possible, how do you explain the feelings we get when something is "not right" or the subliminal warning that alerts us to potential danger? How else would you explain how a school of fish or flight of birds seems to tap into a common awareness and move simultaneously—or how a crowd of people with a common cause often appear as one, as if they were all feeding off one common energy?

Do we actually have the potential to influence the events that affect our lives? Do we create the events in our lives or are we at the mercy of random occurrences? If a herd of animals can tap a common consciousness can we attach ourselves to a desired outcome or are we powerless to determine our reality?

## Power of positive thinking

It took modern visionaries such as Norman Vincent Peale and Dale Carnegie to suggest that the power of positive thinking can change the outcome of events. It took the forward thinking of people like Ram Dass and Deepak Chopra to suggest that we can heal ourselves by changing our way of thinking.

Life exists on many levels and reality can be experienced on many planes as we shall see in the following pages.

How many?

How many do you want?

*Reality is merely an illusion, albeit a very persistent one*—Albert Einstein

# 4

# Levels of reality

How can we be so sure there is more than one level to reality?

Let's begin our search for understanding of this question by examining the physical proof, the model of our universe, the sum total of all matter and physical existence.

## The cosmic dance

First, as has already been suggested, consider that our universe is made up of numerous individual galaxies, each revolving around the other in an orderly, precise celestial harmony, performing a type of cosmic dance.

Within each galaxy we find multitudes of stars moving in balanced relationship with others. Our own Milky Way is a spiral galaxy, a delicate balance of movement within the whole of its defined space.

On the next level we find numerous planets circling their stars in a predictable and disciplined manner, many with numerous moons rotating around them. Each object is provided its own meticulous orbit, held in its place and reliant on all the others by the physics of mass and gravity.

Each planetary environment, in turn has its own cycle we label as years, seasons, night and day. Those that might contain even the simplest of life forms require a delicate balance of all the elements that make up their environments. Each species has its natural predators to ensure that no one becomes dominant and create imbalance.

Then let's consider the basic building block of life and matter: the atom. Although each is different, each has electrons and protons revolving around its nucleus, moving exactly as do the planets and moons around our sun. Within each element are subatomic particles that require a balance and preciseness of their own. Further, scientists suggest that each of these particles is made up of yet smaller universes of matter and so on.

As Eckhart Tolle explains in his book, *The Power of Now*, there is a structure and intelligence at work on even the smallest of levels. He points out that, "a single human cell measuring 1/1,000 of an inch across contains instructions within its DNA that would fill 1,000 books of 600 pages each." [10]

## Co-existence of time

And we haven't even attempted to tackle Einstein's Theory of Relativity which suggests that several aspects of time can co-exist simultaneously . . . or his unified field theory that speaks of ten dimensions that overlap the same physical space. Perhaps one day we will be able to visit what some call *hyperspace*, a concept that has fascinated as well as mystified mystics, magicians, theologians and mathematicians throughout the ages and where Steven Hawkin has said "resides the mind of God."

As you can see by the above illustrations, all of physical creation—physical matter and life itself—exists simultaneously and in repeating patterns. If, then, all of reality occurs concurrently on numerous levels, might it be possible that with enough focused effort we can be conscious of *more* than one level . . . at *one* time?

## What is consciousness?

Consciousness, according to the Third Edition of Webster's New World Dictionary is defined as "an awareness of one's own feelings, what is happening around them or the totality of ones' thoughts and impressions; conscious mind."[11]

But what is it? Where did it come from?

Again, let's go back to the moment of creation. Since the Power that created the universe had to have a consciousness, and since nothing existed until it was created out of the consciousness of this Creator, it follows that all of creation must therefore possess a consciousness. And if all the atoms, the building blocks of physical matter, are conscious, might it all be interconnected somehow; a part of a gigantic "oneness" as would be a grain of sand on a cosmic beach?

Each individual consciousness, of course, varies depending on numerous components such as our emotional makeup, preconceived attitudes and expectations. Since we each view life differently through our individual personalities and points of view based on our own prior experiences, each individual is clearly conscious of a *differing* reality.

As an example, imagine yourself in a small room for a long period of time. While one person might be quite uncomfortable in what he identifies as a claustrophobic environment, a different person might relish the peace and tranquility of a quiet space. Another might focus on the uncomfortable chair in which he is sitting while still someone else is absorbed in the decorative ambience on the surrounding walls. Add music that might evoke a variety of reactions with the residue of the particular activities and emotions of that day, and each person in the room might experience it quite differently.

Another analogy would be that of a stage play. Each night the lighting and sets are in the same places, and there is a constant sound level. The plot never varies and the director has carefully scripted the movements of the actors. However, each critic attending the same performance would view it quite differently and react to it based on the many personal experiences and moods each brings to the theatre on that specific evening.

The more layers of experiences and emotions or consciousness we add to the mix, the more levels of reality will emerge. By considering an event or experience on a multifaceted level rather than as a single piece of sensual input, we are able to heighten our level of consciousness. As a result, our perception of our reality expands as it takes on additional levels of awareness.

And the best part is . . . *it can be changed*, depending on how each of us chooses to view it!

## Changing reality

I recall going to the San Francisco ballet years ago at the request of my wife. Because I would have much rather watched the basketball playoff game on TV, I had resigned myself to expect an extremely dull and boring evening.

It turned out to be pretty much as I expected.

Later that same year, my wife talked me into attending several additional ballet performances with some friends. Having been to one already, I knew I would be in for a few looooong evenings.

As the lights began to dim in the large auditorium, I turned to one of my male buddies seated next to me in order to share a sarcastic remark about wishing to be elsewhere when I noticed a very contented look on his face.

"What are you looking so pleased about?" I asked, quite surprised at his mood.

"Well," he responded with a bit of joy in his voice, "you are sitting in this magnificent Opera House, one of the most beautiful buildings in San Francisco, aren't you? You used to be a building contractor: can't you appreciate the sheer beauty of this place?"

Before I could respond he continued. "And the music . . . we are about to enjoy a classical piece of music performed by 50 very talented musicians. You used to play in the high school band, I'm sure you will be able to relate to the quality of the music when you hear it."

"Well yes but . . ."

"Listen, what you will see on the stage will reflect in motion what you will feel in the music and majesty of this fine old building. Give it a chance . . . let it happen"

You know, he was right. When I experienced the ballet on more than one level and altered my preconceived viewpoint, it became a different experience.

When I combined my reaction to the architectural elegance with the passion of the music and the kaleidoscope of movement on the stage, it became a pleasant blend of sensory input—a multifaceted and expanded reality.

When I changed my expectation of the ballet my preconditioned viewpoint was altered and it became a much more enjoyable experience.

## Different points of view

Now, the skeptic might wonder how changing one's expectations can influence or change the result. How could wishing that the dance was enjoyable make the dancers any better? Isn't that simply reconditioning your mind to accept something that is not really true? Come on . . . a chair is a chair, a fact is a fact, a ballet is a ballet, is it not?

No, if a chair *was* a chair, manufacturers would simplify their catalogue to list only one that would please everyone. The ballet would not vary its format in order to please a wider range of tastes of their patrons. Restaurants would not need to offer a variety of entrees on their menus or ask how you wish your food to be prepared. We would all think that Oreo cookies are a delicacy and that Three Stooges movies are stupid.

Take the example of viewing a glass as being half-full rather than half-empty. If you are not thirsty, the glass has plenty of water in it, but if you live in the desert and the water truck isn't expected to roll into town until next week, the glass suddenly becomes half-empty. The exterior conditions don't change the level in the glass; they just change our perception of it.

## Scientific support

There is some hardcore, scientific evidence that reality can be changed. This is not just fanatical "New Age" whimsy. The quantum physicists, for example, contend that the mere presence of someone *observing* an atom or quark influences its movement or performance. They suggest that all things are energy and as such, are somehow united. Everything interacts with every thing else and nothing acts independently.

If you were to ask the old-style Newtonian scientist the ancient question, "If the tree falls in the forest and there is no one to hear it, does it make a noise?" he might answer, "Of course." However, the more progressive scientist might cast some doubt on this point of view.

The rainforest, indigenous shamans would simplify this concept by suggesting a slightly different perspective. They would contend that our expectation influences our perception and our perception dictates what we term as reality. By holding on to negative thoughts, for example, we attract negative energy.

So if we were to change our viewpoint . . . it's like seeing a ballet with different eyes!

We all know that, don't we? Don't we each color our perspective of "what is" by our current feelings as well as the emotional baggage of past experiences? Add cultural imprints, parental expectations and past life experiences and we form our own distinct, personal viewpoint of reality. Once we own our point of view, it is ours.

So, what can we do to change our reality?

# Modify your reality

When we change our viewpoint we change our reality! When we can let go and release outdated concepts our view of our experiences changes. As soon as I released my prejudicial viewpoint, I began to see the ballet for the beauty of its movement and grace.

We can all do this. Let go of old habitual ways of thinking. A New Age guru might have you sit under a pyramid in order to increase your vibration rate or frequency. A medically trained therapist might want to delve into your sub-conscious to erase or modify that part of your mind that has retained strong personal imprints from a variety of present life experiences. A spiritual master, on the other hand, might desire to guide your super consciousness to a higher plane by first examining your karma or visiting the Akashic records, containing past life memories, found on the astral plane.

A simpler suggestion would be to use some readily available and familiar tools such as meditation, visualization or positive affirmations. Start listening to the inner voice and ignore the negative thoughts. Stop following the familiar pattern of being a victim to justify why something doesn't work for you. Expand your viewpoint to take in the experience on more positive levels. Instead of being angry or fearful of something, examine what created the anger or fear.

External objects or events alone do not define reality. Our individual realities differ and are largely determined by our expectation and experience of them.

Simply change your viewpoint and you change your reality.

> *I don't want to achieve immortality through my work—*
> *I want to achieve it by not dying.* —Woody Allen

# 5

# Reincarnation

If life does have a purpose, and we are individual aspects of this loving and eternal Creative Force, it would stand to reason that we are not only eternal beings but are intended to have a wide variety of experiences while in physical form. What would be the point of partaking in one brief visit to the earth plane and then spending eternity judged on that single transitory encounter?

There are those who maintain that since the Bible does not refer to reincarnation, it must not exist. I submit that this issue might be clearer when you study how and by whom the final version of the modern day Bible was assembled.

## Ancient manuscripts

It is well known that for the first three centuries following the death of Jesus of Nazareth, the political rulers of Rome persecuted the early Christians. Then, following Emperor Constantine's sudden conversion, Christianity became the prevailing religion of the powerful Roman Empire. When their interpretation of the canon conflicted with that of Alexandria and Constantinople, Rome's domination of the ecumenical council assembled in AD 367 led to the creation of what we know as the New Testament.

Not only did the editors apparently intentionally exclude those stories and concepts that did not support their view, but some would suggest that they might well have modified them to suit the political needs of the church authorities of that day. Add to that the failing eyesight of the scribes, inaccurate translation or simply embellishments and changes made to support the doctrinal or theological beliefs of those in charge, and we just might have been provided a collection of specific narratives that contain a bias toward the Roman point of view.

Recently discovered manuscripts, such as the Codex, Sinaticus, written around 340 AD and discovered in the Greek Orthodox monastery of St Catherine of Alexandria by German scholar Constantin Tischendorf in 1859, bears this out. [12] In addition, the existence of a large body of Gnostic writings such as the *Gnostic Gospel of Thomas*, found in a cave in Nag Hammadi, Egypt in 1945 supports this theory as well. These, as well as other excluded texts, suggest that the New Testament might well have been edited and embellished for political and doctrinal reasons.

Clement of Alexandria, an early Church father, wrote that Jesus had secret teachings not recorded in the Gospels and that they were intended only for those who were initiated into the great mysteries. Were these early teachings banned or destroyed by the Orthodox Church because it disagreed with them? Could it be possible that the early church leaders, not unlike some of the present day governments, did not tell us the entire story?

Why would the early church withhold this information from us?

## Power of the church

History reminds us that for the past 2000 years in Europe, the Church has competed with the numerous ruling monarchies of Europe for power. They held on to their supremacy, not by amassing large regiments of soldiers or taxing the population, but by holding the keys to eternal redemption. By creating a mystique around the spiritual knowledge that they alone possessed, they would be able to hold sway over the people.

One means by which the early church leaders did this was to teach that God's eternal judgment is based solely on our one, single experience here on earth. If we were thought to be sinners or were to die without proper repentance that only the church could provide, we might denied permanent citizenship in Heaven. To suggest that we could find our own way on our own or that we could come back in a later life to make amends would certainly minimize their authority over the population. However, to advocate that following their doctrine was the *only* path to eternal salvation, the Church could successfully compete, or even co-exist, with the powerful royal monarchs of the day.

## An argument for reincarnation

A powerful argument for reincarnation is to ask yourself this question: why would compassionate God would provide us only one shot at a physical life experience and base our "foreverness" on just one earthly experience? What would be His motivation to have created, say, a black child centuries ago to suffer the indignities, hard life and painful death as a slave and yet create another who is born into privilege, health and wealth? Would a compassionate God have us "burn in Hell" for one mistake? Would we be excluded from Heaven because we failed to discover the necessary guidelines for salvation in one short stay here?

In the third century, Origen of Alexandria taught that we are responsible for what we are and that everything that happens to us is a result of our actions and motives. He suggested that all the good things or bad things that occur are the consequences of *all* our past lives. He believed that "karma," or the law of cause and effect, basically reaping what you sow, provided an explanation for the apparent inequality of the circumstances of each soul.

The preexistence of the soul could be illustrated in the Old Testament story of Jacob and Esau. God reported that he loved Jacob and hated Esau even before they were born. This would suggest that either they did something in the womb to make God angry or that it was a past life to which the Divinity was referring.

But even without this historical testimony, simple observation of nature would demonstrate this notion of reincarnation in the natural life/death/rebirth cyclical nature of the universe. Seasons begin and end only to begin again the following year. Tides rise and fall over and over again. Rain falls only to be used, discarded and eventually purified and recycled back to the planet. The seed of each family is eventually passed on to the next generation. Many species of animals, such as the trout in the streams of the Northwest, give up their lives to spawn in order that rebirth might reoccur. We breathe in oxygen and exhale carbon oxide which is then transformed back into oxygen by the rainforests, which we breathe in, only to exhale once more, and the process repeats. Even the Earth itself struggles to repair and regenerate itself after man does his best to wreak wide-scale destruction.

## Redemption

Having fallen from grace, might not this reincarnation concept be a means for mankind to regain our point of origin—our oneness with God? As an unconscious portion of His totality, is it possible that we have been given the opportunity or, perhaps, the assignment to experience all there is in life and to permanently return to the One Source when our mission has been completed? Are we not, after all, God, the Creator, experiencing Himself/Herself in physical form?

As adults we learn from our past mistakes. History is a great teacher of what works and what doesn't. By this same token, if we could learn from our past lives, could we not cut to the chase and get on with our higher purpose?

Hummmm ... I wonder if it is possible ...

> *You miss 100% of the shots you never take.* —Wayne Gretzky, hockey player

# 6

# Creating our own experience

If, God is pure energy, then, and everything that exists is an expression of this God energy, might we be an aspect of God experiencing reality in physical form—a part of this Creator Spirit? If this is so, might we not to some extent be co-creators as well? After all, if God is a creator and we are made in His image and in His likeness, then as spiritual beings we must be creators of our individual experiences. And as creators, it would follow that we can change our experiences.

How do we do this? We do this by knowing that the proverbial glass is half full rather than half empty. We alter our reality when we experience the ballet as a combination of pleasant sensory experiences rather than a boring waste of time. We create a new experience by adopting a different perception of what we previously labeled as our previous reality.

## Levels of consciousness

Since mystics throughout time have taught that each of us is a reflection of our multi-level experiences and lifetimes, and since science has demonstrated that there may possibly be numerous levels of reality, from atoms to solar systems, there emerges a pattern that suggests that there is more than one level of consciousness as well.

Certainly when we realize that our waking consciousness is separate from that of God's, we cannot deny at least two distinct levels of consciousness—His and ours.

Now let's factor in another sphere of consciousness—that which the Western-trained psychologist might refer to as our *sub*-conscious. This is the hidden, underlying part of us that robotically reacts in predictable ways due to our preconditioning. Take the simple process of breathing. We instinctively take in air and exhale carbon dioxide, thanks to direction from a deep level of sub-conscious operating on automatic pilot. When we walk, we don't think about lifting one heel and bending the knee and rotating off the toes, etc. In fact, think about walking and notice how difficult it becomes when you attempt to individually coordinate all the necessary movements.

Then there is a higher, super or collective conscious. This is the plane accessible by large groups of similar thinking human beings such as "think tanks" working on a common problem. This is the energy created in a football stadium when the fans become of one mind. This is the power that is created when the population of an entire nation possesses a common cause uniting them.

Didn't Christ tell us that there is a powerful force when two or more come together in His name?

## The Eastern view

If we were to look at the levels of consciousness from the view of yoga or Vedic philosophy, we would discover not three but five separate "sheaths" or body consciousnesses.

The first is the physical or dense body, the one with which we often identify ourselves and are the most familiar. It is the vehicle by which we get around when in physical form and what reflects back to us in the mirror. This is the consciousness that keeps the heart pumping and lungs working when we are preoccupied with other things.

The next is the bio-energetic body or life force energy that Yoga refers to as Prana. In Western parlance it might be called the soul or spirit. It is the consciousness that carries the past life memories and has knowledge of our higher purpose and why we are here.

A third level of awareness we each possess is our sensory body; that portion of us that reasons and feels based on the perception of our five senses. It is separate from the intellect or ego mind, or what some may call the left-brain reasoning part of us.

Independent from that which reacts to what we perceive is our intuitive body or higher mind. It is the level of consciousness that we call our wisdom and higher intelligence and is the means by which we discriminate between right and wrong.

Lastly we have the higher self, where we connect to Samadhi or the Divine Source. It is what is often referred to as transcendental consciousness. Might this be the level of awareness that would explain angel sightings or extraterrestrial visitations, unexplainable by empirical science, as recorded in the mystical traditions of countless cultures?

And who is to say that the above models are a complete list?

## Expanding consciousness

It is believed by some that early spiritual initiates of Egypt sought to expand their consciousness by being challenged in secret rituals at temples along the headwaters of the Nile in order to open and awaken their *kundalini*. They believed that enlightenment would be accomplished by raising the vibration of the nerve centers similar to the Indian/yogic concept known as *Chakras* located along the spine. It was a serious commitment, as only those devoted neophytes who survived the long ordeal and were found to be worthy were initiated into the Mystery Schools whose ultimate purpose was to protect and maintain knowledge of the secrets of the universe.

Of course, one cannot exclude followers of some of the more *far out* groups, such as the *Order of Melchizedek*, each claiming that theirs is the way, the true order of the divine Hierarchy that exist throughout the solar systems and is the repository of the *true* knowledge.

Most of all these belief systems and organizations would no doubt argue that because there are many levels of existence, how could it not be true of consciousness as well? If we came from the loins of the Ultimate consciousness that knows no boundaries, why would we be relegated to a realm of consciousness that has limited and impenetrable boundaries when we take on a physical form? Is not our universe expanding as we speak?

## Dreaming

Dreaming is undeniably yet another level of consciousness. When we dream, our reality at that moment shifts from the sleeping body that is conscious of breathing, digesting and a myriad of survival functions to that of the experience of the dream. When we awaken, we often dismiss it as "just a dream," but is it? At the moment you were dreaming it was real, wasn't it? Does it make the experience less valid to know that it was not what we refer to as waking consciousness? In fact, in many ways a dream is more real than waking life in that it delivers useful information without the restrictions of waking life.

We get valuable messages in our dreams—if only we take the time to listen. Einstein, known primarily for the scientific knowledge he developed from his logical reasoning mind, derived the equation for the conversion of mass to energy from a dream.

The book *Dr. Jekyll and Mr. Hyde*, was inspired by a dream. Julius Howe saw the details of the sewing machine in a dream. It is said that Robert Fulton invented the steam engine as a result of dream.

## Understanding the symbols

We can all gain value from these often-nonsensical nocturnal visual images of this alternate consciousness. There are countless examples of how understanding the symbols in a dream provide life-changing messages, if only the dreamer will listen and pay attention. For example, if one dreams about losing something such as a wallet, purse or keys, the dream probably is speaking to one's identity. The dreamer may wish to consider where in his life he has lost some part of his self worth or esteem.

Fear of falling in a dream might suggest an attempt to hold on to an outmoded concept whereas a fun flying dream might confirm a smooth flight through life. Although dying in a dream could be a precognitive experience, it generally suggests that some aspect of the dreamer's life is dying off, such as an old attitude or relationship. In any case, examine the people or places in a dream and make an association with regard to your feeling about it or them. For example, if you had a dream that you are being driven in a car to a specific destination, you might want to examine the *feeling* you have about the driver and the place you are headed. Most often the objects in a dream are only symbols and not intended to be literal representations of people or places

Once you get the hang of it, dreams can provide answers to specific problems you present to your dream self before you drift off to sleep. Incubate your question and see what kind of answer you receive. It could come to you in a specific dream or it might be revealed in some portion of your waking life.

Since dreams seem to have few limitations they also take on many forms. In precognitive or clairvoyant dreams we may be presented with information about the future or know about events not experienced in waking life. In a telepathic dreams or shared dream we may connect with others. Past life dreams may provide insight learned in previous incarnations and a visitation dream may bring the wisdom of our ancestral spirits.

## Shaman dreaming

My wife and I have traveled extensively to many indigenous cultures and spent time with mystical shamans who receive insight from their dreams. In fact, many of these spiritual leaders believe that dreams are, in actuality, *true* reality because what we refer to as waking life has so many limitations. They point out that when we dream we are free to be or do anything we want. Unrestricted by time or gravity or earthbound rules, *dreamtime* proves access to the unfettered world of the spirits as well as other dimensions and levels of reality not accessible in the waking state. They contend that we all can do this and in fact we often do; we just dismiss our experience as "a dream" and therefore a meaningless nighttime fantasy.

They are often quick to remind us that our only limitations are those that we impose on ourselves.

We have witnessed firsthand mystic healers from remote regions of the world enter an altered or dream state to visit the "lower world" to retrieve a power animal or to speak to a deceased ancestor spirit for spiritual guidance. Many cultures rely on the dreams of their shamans to heal their sick and provide guidance to the tribe.

On more than one occasion we were met at the edge of a village by shamans who know we were coming because their dreams told them. One knew we were approaching because the spirits of the trees warned of our arrival in his *day dream*. Another claimed to be aware we were on our way because the shaman from an adjoining village spoke of our intentions to visit in his previous night's dream.

Is this ability only limited to the few who have learned some special secret technique?

Anthony Shafton in his book, *Dream-Singers: Night Dreams in African-American Life*, [13] states that 70% of African-Americans he interviewed claimed to have had one or more visitation from a deceased relative. And this is not just from the elders of the family. Even in the 18 to 35 year old category, more than 2/3 have received information, a warning or an assurance that they believe was from an ancestor. It is interesting to note that only 1/3 of the whites have reported such an occurrence which, he concludes, suggests that basic belief systems within races and cultures would explain the differences in reported experiences.

If we changed our belief system could we alter our reality?

## Living in the dreamtime

Dr. Stanley Krippner, a world recognized authority on shamanism agrees that the indigenous shamans believe that we all live in the dreamtime and that *all* things dream. He states that since dreams are energy images they can be heard, if only we knew how to listen. He claims that dreams are a part of the natural rhythm of life and their essences can be perceived.

Dr. Peggy Grove, a leading expert in aboriginal rock art, reports that many of the original Australian creation stories that have been handed down from one generation to the next suggest that the world was created through the dream of the Creator Force. According to some versions, the world was initially flat until the ancestor beings dreamed the landscape into existence. In fact, they speak of how conception of a new human life begins with the dream of the father, who dreams his dream into his wife at the moment of conception. The ancients believed that they literally dream their children into existence.

Dr. Jeremy Narby, an anthropologist and conservationist demonstrates the convergence between shamanic knowledge and "real science" in his book, *The Cosmic Serpent*. Having spent much of his time in the rainforests with the shamans, he believes that there are many levels of reality and that spiritual intelligence and dreaming inhabits all levels. He suggests that everything is animated with consciousness and therefore we can be connected with it. Therefore, waking awareness, dreams, as well as plants, animals and deceased relatives are all interconnected. To limit our belief is to limit our experience.

Dr. Robert Bosnic, a well-known Jungian therapist and author of *A Little Course In Dreams*, states that the dream is not only powerful, it is an independent "energy," separate from our individual cultural notions. He wonders, "What if we were to perceive that dreams had a voice? What if we decided to listen to the dream – experience it - rather than assume its only message is in the interpretation of its symbols?"

Gotta believe

Fortunately, there are still a few societies who still believe in their dreams. My wife and I were fortunate to have spent a day with a Karo shaman from one of the small tribal villages in Ethiopia's outback. When we inquired as to this shaman healer's spiritual beliefs, he cautiously parroted what he thought we wanted to hear: the story of a White Man-God who died on large wooden sticks just as it is taught by visiting missionary groups. But, after gaining his trust, and assuring him that we were not evangelists, he slowly shared that his truth comes by way of his dreams. In fact, he told us that everyone in the village gets their truth in this way.

These people believe that their departed ancestors visit them each night from a higher plain in order to provide specific spiritual as well as practical direction to their daily life. As a result, they know where to locate the otherwise elusive game, or are alerted to pending droughts.

"The ancient ones guide us," we were told.

One of the most recognizable means we all can partake of this readily available spiritual communication is through this same process of recognizing and acting upon our dreams. This means of communication is common among the dwindling numbers of indigenous tribal communities in the more inaccessible portions of our planet.

Most often, the shaman will interpret his or the dreams of others to guide those seeking his advice. In other cultures, a single village shaman speaks with his departed relatives for the benefit of the entire tribe. Some are said to gain information by communing with nature spirits from whom they receive direction to assure their continuing existence.

The South American Jivaro shaman will even classify his dreams into three categories. The first is the positive, or *kuntuknar* dream, and usually involves tribal life having to do with hunting. The shaman keeps this dream to himself. To share it takes away its power.

The second dream of the Jivaro is the *mesekramper* dreams, which are the "bad" dreams. These, according to the dreamer, need to be shared with as many as possible in order that they defuse the power.

The third type of dream and the most powerful, are the *Karampar* dreams. These are the dreams that allow the shaman to converse with the spirit world directly.

Shaman have even been known to extend this communicate beyond directives from spirits and to communicate amongst themselves by way of their dreams. On the Serengeti plains of Africa we were shown a large communal rock which, when beat by a shaman, will allow him to connect with other shaman from neighboring tribes in their dreams.

## Community Dreaming

However, psychic dreaming is not limited just to shamans. Many indigenous cultures live by the messages of the dream. Most commonly it is the patriarch of the household who performs the dreaming for the entire family. However, the head of each family unit of the Achuar tribe in the Eastern Amazon of Ecuador, for example, wakes at 3:00 AM each morning to drink a bitter substance so that he might first purge the negative energy from his body. After becoming violently ill, he will spend the remainder of each morning interpreting the dreams of the male members of the family.

Sometimes the entire village gets into the act. The men, women and children of the Senoi people of Malaysia rely on the information brought to each of them in their nighttime dreams. You would meet major resistance if you were to argue with them that the waking state was the "true reality."

## The Conception Dream

Dr. Stephen Aizenstat, Dean of the Pacifica Graduate Institute in Santa Barbara, California, tells the story of a tribe in East Africa in which the birthday of a child is not counted from the day of its physical birth, nor even the day of conception. For them, the birthday is the first time the child is a dream in its mother's mind!

Aware of her intention to conceive a child with a particular father, the mother goes off to sit alone under a tree. There she sits and listens until she can hear the song of the child she hopes to conceive. Once she has "heard" or dreamed it, she returns to her village and teaches it to the father so that they can sing it to together as they make love--inviting the child to join them.

After the child is conceived, she sings to the baby in her womb. Then she teaches the song to the old women and midwives of the village so that throughout the labor and at the miraculous moment of birth itself, the child is greeted with its song.

After the birth, all the villagers learn the song of their new member and, later, sing to the child when it falls or hurts itself. It is sung at times of triumph, or in rituals and initiations. This song becomes a part of the marriage ceremony when the child is grown. And, at the end of life, his or her loved ones will gather around the deathbed and sing this song for the last time.

## The power of the dream

Some creative dreamers have even learned how to "lucid dream." Lucid dreaming is the ability to be conscious that you are dreaming and become the observer self, observing the dream. One is able to move into the ego of the dream-self and confront the monster that is chasing him or cross over the barrier that keeps him from his goal. Once can not only overcome the challenges that are being presented in the dream but can also explore and learn from the messages that are being presented by the higher self.

How is this possible?

Since the Creator Force created all original matter from a conscious thought or dream, all things—every rock and drop of water, every creature and life form in the Universe—are elements or images of that original dream. In effect, we are dreamers in the dreamscape of the Creator's dream. Being the dreamer and the dream at the same time, then, it would stand to reason that we can enter the dream as does the lucid dreamer and change the dream to our liking. [14]

But where do we go when we dream? Does our consciousness actually travel somewhere such as might be described by those who claim to be able to go out-of-body? This might explain how we can wake up with the resolution to the problems we have incubated prior to the sleep state or meet the dream egos of others to work to a common cause.

You want to be able to do this?

If the answer is yes . . . then do it!

> In the depth of winter I finally learned that within me there lay an invincible summer. —Albert Camus

# 7

# Co-creators with God

If we are co-creators with God, why in the world would we create all the problems, sickness and misery that are so prevalent on this earth?

## The original sin

Some Christian theologians might suggest that it has to do with the fall from grace resulting from Eve's bite of the infamous apple in the Garden of Eden. According to the Book of Genesis, the first two residents on this planet had been the perfect creation. They must have been pleasing to the Supreme Being because they had been provided full access to all that existed in Heaven and on earth—everything, that is, except the forbidden fruit from the tree of the knowledge of good and evil.

"Of every tree of the garden thou mayest freely eat," God specifically instructed them, "but of the tree of the knowledge of good and evil thou shalt not eat of it: for in the day that thou eatest thereof thou shalt surely die."

One day a serpent appeared to Eve and asked her why she did not eat from *all* the trees in the garden? Eve responded by stating that one of the primary edicts from Headquarters specifically forbade her from eating from the tree of knowledge. She added that this directive appeared to be somewhat non-negotiable.

The serpent quickly rebuffed her saying, "Ye shall not surely die: for God doth know that the day ye eat thereof, then your eyes shall be opened." She could be as a God, the serpent went on to suggest, full of all the knowledge that was easily within her reach. After all, he chided, why would it be there if it were not intended to be eaten and enjoyed?

## Falling from grace

The moment this specific decree from God was disobeyed, everything is said to have changed. With this one bite came the loss of innocence and virtue. The Bible suggests that the day in which Eve was disobedient to her Creator was the day she, and all those who were to follow, fell from favor. In claiming the power to be our own God, mankind lost the special bond it had with the Creator Force. In becoming so enamored with ego and the physical sensations and pleasures that exist in the physical realm we are told that we began the journey away from the subtler spiritual plane that was to be our intended inheritance.

But having been formed in the image of God, perhaps each of us has retained the ability to create our own individual reality. If we were to look to the spiritual knowing we each possess at the inner most depths of our soul, might we find our own path to this higher understanding and awareness? Unfortunately, the Western world too often seems preoccupied with the trappings of the material world.

Each succeeding generation strives to measure personal success by material gain and personal power and with it the inevitable loss of the memory from whence we came.

According to the Biblical text, this rebellion to the way and word of God was not exclusively confined to just the physical world. It is said that Lucifer, one of the angels holding court in God's inner circle, led a mutiny that cast him and his followers to the "lower world." Desiring to be his own boss, he too was stripped of his exalted status and became separated from the Creator.

Whether you are a Biblical literalist or prefer to believe the Bible stories are simplified replications of man's increasing spiritual blindness, the result appears to be the same. We are spiritual lambs who have lost our way.

How do we find our way back?

If we perceive this fallout as original sin, which must be rectified, might there not be some means to make amends? After all, Adam and Eve were rookies, new at this material world stuff. Isn't our God a forgiving God?

## Choices

So how do we find our way back? Well, it depends on who you talk to!

Some teachers of *Eastern thought* might have us simply realign our chakras with the seven planes of being. By balancing the natural forces of energy that course through our body we might reach common thought with the Creative force.

*Indigenous shaman* might remove or transform what they see as disruptive or negative energy that has prevented us from receiving pure thought. If we were to remove the dis-ease that blocks our ability to reach the dream world, we would have access to a higher plane of being.

*Conservative Orthodox Christians* in old-fashioned healing revival tents might claim that the way to salvation is to physically cast out one's personal devils. This, they suggest, requires complete submission to the Holy Spirit in order to restore "the Light." After all, they might point out, wasn't Saul of Tarsus, a man dedicated to the persecution of the early Christians, converted on the road to Damascus with "the light?" He is said to have encountered a blinding radiance from Heaven, above the brightness of the sun, shining all around him. By changing his ways he became a different person and was saved from eternal damnation.

## Assistance from the Ascended Masters

*Ancient alchemists*, on the other hand, might transform the nature of ordinary metals into a powerful spiritual tool in order to reach higher thought and salvation. They were said to have mastered a mysterious process involving the use of the powerful rays and energies of celestial bodies. They used an all-consuming fire they called a violet transmuting flame, in order to activate the wisdom of what they called "the Seventh Ray."

*The Great White Brotherhood* is an organization thought by many to consist of many of the Ascended Masters, including Melchizedek, Jesus, Enoch, Elijah and Elisha who are said to use similar metaphysical processes to achieve healings, miracles and prophecies. By amplifying the violet flame of the Holy Spirit through their auras, they claim to be able to transmute the darkness of ignorance into the light of understanding. Many followers of Saint Germain believe he is using this same seventh-ray flame while in spiritual form to light the way for all those who might lead us as we move from the old millennium into the so-called enlightened New Age.

Origen of Alexandria, one of the early Christian theologians who suffered during the Decian persecution (AD 250-251), [15]also believed that the creation of the material world was the *result* of the fall from grace. But believing in reincarnation, he taught early Christians that Christ's message was that our salvation is in the *eternal* now, not this physical life. His message was that we can re-ascend to our former state of unity with God by conquering temptations until the soul becomes virtuous.

Sort of a "do it again and again until you get it right"?

Trial and error

These thoughts are not dissimilar from those of countless others who have followed the words of various sages, avatars and Ascended Masters throughout history. They suggest that we have free will and can have anything that we want in this or any other lifetime because, after all, we are creators of our experiences. Many make a strong case for reincarnation, contending that after lifetimes of chasing after the false gods of earthly power and material gain, we will finally wake up to discover the spiritual inheritance that awaits us all!

It can't really be that simple . . .

. . . can it?

> *Here is a test to see if your mission on earth is finished.
> If you are alive, it isn't*—Francis Bacon

# 8

# Taking Action for Change

Ok... all of that is fine... but if it is true that we create our reality, why are our lives in such turmoil? If we manifest everything that takes place in our lives, why in the world don't we have peace on earth, perfect health, or cell phones that don't drop calls? In a perfect world, shouldn't we be able to get everything that we want?

It is, of course, a fair question to wonder why, if we can control our destiny, our life is less than we might wish it to be. Why do we purposely create situations that cause us emotional or physical pain?

## A case in point

A letter I recently received from an unhappily married woman in her thirties addressed this very issue. She is a mother of two children, trapped in an unfulfilled marriage. She was concerned that not only was her life not working, but that three psychics on separate occasions had suggested the same specific course of action that turned out to be a personal disaster.

She wrote that I, along with two other psychics, each independently affirmed that her tentative plan to relocate her family to her hometown in Colorado and enter into a family business partnership would be a "good move." So, bolstered with what she interpreted to be three separate and positive directives, she uprooted her husband and children and moved in with her mother.

Her letter went on to explain that although she knew nothing about her family's real estate business, she assumed that she had obtained adequate confirmation that moving her household and changing her career would be a positive step. In fact, she confided that although she never really got along with her mother, the mandate received from her three metaphysical advisors would provide her with the happiness she so desperately sought.

Boy, was she in for a shock!

It turned out to be, in her words, "a total disaster on every level!" Soon after her arrival, her newborn son required surgery. She complained that her kids were miserable, her husband was unable to find a job and everyone hated the weather. Not only were there numerous family crises, but she found that she didn't get along with her mom. In addition, what she perceived was going to be an easy job in her mom's real estate business turned out to be a bust, as she never sold a single house. And to top the whole thing off, her expensive house in California was still without a buyer.

She moved back home and is much happier now. She stated that now that she has returned, she and her husband have found fulfilling jobs, her children are much happier and healthier, and the house looks better than ever. Although she acknowledged that she had dealt positively with some old issues with her mom, the move was terrible in every other sense of the word.

She ended her letter by asking how *three* psychics who professed to be able to read the future could be so wrong? How could each reading confirm that returning to live with her mom would be a good move when it obviously was the complete opposite? She was at a total loss as to how we could read this as "great" when in fact, it turned out to be a living nightmare.

## Misinterpretation

There are, of course numerous reasons why this situation could have occurred; the first and obvious one being that all three of us could simply have been wrong. Not even the best psychics in the world are correct all the time. But to have more than one of us come to the same "inaccurate" conclusion might be more than a simple coincidence.

Another explanation would be that since things are always in flux, world shattering extraneous events such as the 9/11 disaster could alter what might otherwise occur on the individual level. Since a Universal Consciousness exists that is more powerful than any individual's ability to counteract it, a greater collective energy force can very well dictate events beyond anyone's ability to modify them.

A third option is that she might have self destructed because of some past or present life event. It's the old "what goes around comes around" and "we reap what we sow" concept that suggests that what may have taken place was some sort of karmic payback for a prior action.

A fourth possibility could have been that her predetermined point of view may have created her dilemma. When we hold onto personal negative attitudes we, in effect, influence or create the outcome. Since our expectations greatly influence our perceptions, by maintaining a pessimistic notion such as "things never seem to work out," we can easily derail an intellectually desired outcome.

Although it could also be explained as mental telepathy between psychics or simply that she heard only what she wanted to hear, there is yet another possibility that is more common than you might realize and that applies to *this* situation.

## Confronting karma

However, we need to keep in mind that we often manifest what we need to experience. We often create situations, events and relationships that relate to the reason we are here in physical form on Planet Earth. Since we are an extension, as it were, of the Creator Spirit, and because there appears to be a master plan and balance to the universe and all of creation, everything we experience is for some sort of higher purpose often beyond our limited or self-serving perception. Simply put, we experience what we need to in order to grow spiritually or, in the words of the Eastern religions, resolve past karma.

When we look more closely at this woman's experience, we notice that her tribulations have a common theme. All of her problems began the moment she moved back to her family. What she expected to be a retreat to the safety of her family home and mom's business was, instead, an opportunity to confront and resolve some personal and family issues. Often what we perceive to be a "problem" is, in actuality, an opportunity to confront some personal karma that can best be resolved while in physical form. The direction we receive from a higher source is most often an opportunity for spiritual growth.

After all, isn't that what we came here to do?

> What lies behind us and what lies before us are tiny matters compared to what lies within us. —Ralph Waldo Emerson

# 9

# Predictions of the future

If we are co-creators of our experiences and are apparently provided with free will, how are the self-proclaimed psychics who hang out in the psychic chat rooms and on the front pages of the *National Enquirer* able to predict future events? Is the future so set in stone that we are unable to change it?

There are, of course, a number of well-documented predictions in numerous ancient cultures and religious manuscripts that warn us of things to come.

## The Bible

The Old Testaments of the Christian Bible contains copious stories involving information provided through Jewish seers called *Nabhi*, or "called persons," warning the population of events to come. The powerful King Nebuchadnezzar of Babylon kidnapped Daniel from Jerusalem to interpret his prophetic dreams.[16] Joseph, of multicolored dream coat fame, successfully interpreted the dream of an Egyptian pharaoh predicting the seven years of feast and famine. Other Biblical seers such as Jeremiah, Habakkuk and Ezekiel seemingly foretold many future events including the downfall of Assyria, Babylonia and Judah. [17]

The New Testament contains many stories of futuristic revelations as well. Angels informed the wise men of the pending birth of a messiah and later instructed Mary to escape to Egypt to avoid the killing of his new son. Christ appeared to have been forewarned of his pending fate through his direct line connection to a Higher Consciousness and the Book of Revelations is full of predictions concerning *the last days*.

By way of dreams, meditation or prayer, spiritual insight appears to be accessible by those selected to receive this divine inspiration or those simply savvy enough to know how to tap into it.

## The Oracle of Delphi

Over 2,500 years ago, the Oracle of Delphi was said to have made predictions for famous kings and generals who would make the arduous journey to the remote mountaintop in Greece to seek a peek into the future. Battles and conquests were plotted based on the predictions of the future by these young female seers. Originally called the daughters of Python, the mythological serpent son of Gaia, or Mother Earth, the Oracles gained their insight by entering a trance-like state induced by eating laurel leaves and inhaling the fumes emitted from an underground subterranean cave.

In mythology, Zeus originally selected this sacred site by commissioning two eagles to locate the navel or center of the earth. Zeus marked the spot with a sacred stone that, as the story goes, became the seat upon which the young oracles of antiquity sat while counseling those who sought their wisdom.

Later, the God Apollo apparently got into the act. History records the influence of the god Apollo-Pythias who witnessed numerous conquests of Delphi by foreign nations for control of the power of these young mystics.

Did these metaphysical maidens actually predict the future? Or, perhaps as many have suggested, the Oracles may have merely provided encouragement to those seeking power to fulfill their destiny?

There is a wonderful story that the king of Lydia (560-540 BC) traveled to Delphi to inquire if he would be victorious in a proposed war against the Persians. He was told "Croesus, having crossed the river Halys, will destroy a great kingdom." [18] He followed what he assumed to be his destiny only to be defeated by Cyrus the Great and taken prisoner. When he was released years later he visited the Oracle of Delphi and complained about having received a prediction that was not true.

He was informed that the prediction was indeed true: it was the downfall of a great kingdom—his!

## Nostradamus

The well-known 16th century psychic Nostradamus (1503-1566) claimed to have received his insight from an angelic spirit. Aided by a broad understanding of astrological knowledge, he reached his higher state of consciousness by focusing his attention on the elements of fire or water. This, accentuated by mild hallucinogens such as nutmeg in order to enhance his visions, brought instant notoriety to this innovative physician healer.

Was he able to predict the future? Take for example, what some claim is his prediction of the rise and fall of Hitler in Century 2, Quantrain 24: [19]

> Beasts ferocious with hunger will cross the rivers,
> The greater part of the battlefield will be against *Hister*.
> Into a cage of iron will the great one be drawn,
> When the child of Germany observes nothing.

Is "Hister" a misspelling of the notorious Hitler or does it perhaps refer to a geographical region near the Danube River, near Hitler's birthplace? Is the cage of iron a modern day tank seen through the eyes of a 16th century Frenchman?

Or from Nostradamus' Almanac of 1557:

> The shocking and infamous armed one will fear the great furnace,
> First the chosen one, the captives not returning:
> The world's lowest crime, the Angry Female Irale not at ease,
> Barb, Hister, Malta, and the Empty One does not return.

Does this refer to the plight of the Jewish people during the Holocaust? Is "Irale" a misspelling of Israel?

In Century 1, Quatrain 35, some would suggest that death of King Henry II of France was foretold in the following verse:

> "The young lion will overcome the older one,
> One the field of combat in a single battle;
> He will pierce his eyes through a golden cage,
> Two wounds made one, then he dies a cruel death."

In June 1559, Henry II participated in a jousting tournament against the Comte de Montgomery. Both combatants used shields with lion emblems and Henry suffered two wounds in his eye and suffered an agonizing death. Was this an accurate prediction of demise of Henry II or a general statement that could be conveniently applied to this somewhat unimportant moment in the larger scheme of things?

Nostradamus' supporters claim that the predictions were so frightening that he purposefully disguised them to be mysterious. Detractors argue that because they were so full of metaphors and anagrams and not listed in historical sequence they can only be considered coincidental, at best.

## The Book of Revelation

When we look at the Biblical book of Revelation, scholars provide a variety of interpretations of what was meant by the writer believed to have been John the Apostle. Many theologians view the descriptions as being a literal visual report of the apocalypse or the end of the world using the available references familiar to the writer of that day. Supporters of this argument make a strong case by paralleling the early events in these chapters to current world circumstances.

Others argue that the visions, as frightening and mysterious as they are, can be interpreted to describe almost every disaster through history. Perhaps it was not meant to suggest the end of the world but to provide an immediate warning to the early Christians in preparation for the suffering they were to experience at the hands of the conquering Roman overlords. Since the center of the known world at that time was primarily what we know as the Middle East, perhaps the stories pertained to the future struggles of just the countries in that region.

## Edgar Cayce

A few have even suggested that the religious text was intended to be symbolic or, perhaps, the esoteric images one might encounter in a dream. Edgar Cayce (1877-1945), perhaps the best known prophet of modern times, postulated that the seven churches mentioned in the narrative might be interpreted as the seven spiritual centers or chakras of the body; the four beasts as the four lower spiritual center's desires; the 24 elders are the 24 cranial nerves that lead to the five senses, and so on. As each spiritual center is opened, he postulated, the body is purified and a higher spirituality can be realized.

Cayce, often referred to as the "sleeping prophet," received his information from what modern psychologists might call a self-induced sleep or hypnotic trance. Although he provided a few predictions of the future, his most notable pronouncements involved thousands of medical diagnoses, reportedly in the 85 to 90 percent accuracy range. His well-documented readings also provided information on a wide range of subjects from personal past life karma readings to esoteric information regarding the construction methods and significance of the mystic properties of the Great Pyramid [20]

He did predict terrible worldwide disasters that were to take place in the closing decades of the twentieth century that would result in great earth upheavals and flooding. It is true that we have had a greater frequency of earthquakes and volcano eruptions than ever before. There is no question that weather patterns are changing and that the deterioration of the ozone layer and global warming are cause for concern.

Is this what he saw and misinterpreted the timing? Or perhaps his warning was to allow us to make changes to avoid what will occur if we do not take direct action?

## The third secret of Fatima

There has been much written about the claims of the three shepherd children who reportedly received warnings in visions from the Madonna in Fatima, Portugal in 1917. It is said that the first was a prediction that a worse war (World War II?) would follow the war that was underway in Europe at the time. A second revelation called for piety and the eventual consecration of Russia. The third has remained a secret to this day and has been speculated to be either a prediction of the end of the line of popes or some sort of apocalypse at the end of the last millennium.

Does this portend the appearance of the Anti Christ? Dr. Gerald Larue, a professor emeritus of religion at the University of Southern California suggests in his book, *The supernatural, the Occult and the Bible*, that the visions were only "childish hallucinations" while others speculate that they were predictions of things to come. Could the 1981 assassination attempt on Pope John Paul, the advent of global warming or the 9/11 attack and subsequent worldwide terrorist activity be the fulfillment of this prophecy? Perhaps the collective consciousness of the world will be strong enough to prevent a cataclysmic apocalyptic war or a catastrophe of worldwide proportions.

When we examine these and the many other "predictions" we are left with more questions than answers. Can the future be predicted? And if so, does the forecast in Revelations actually predict the end of the world? Were Edgar Cayce, Nostradamus and the children in Portugal correct when they spoke of the pending disaster for this planet in their pronouncements?

Let's look into a few of the myths and legends of ancient cultures for additional insight.

> *If a man does not keep pace with his companions, perhaps it is because he hears a different drummer.* —Henry David Thoreau

# 10

# The indigenous myths

Ok... so a few predictions may have actually turned out to have some semblance of truth to them. But what about the many forecasts of the future uttered by metaphysicians of every stripe, from recognized spiritualists and mystic seers to so-called roadside carnival fortune tellers that have failed to materialize? How is it that if they have the ability to "see" the future, many of their predictions turn out to be incorrect? Does this mean the so-called psychics, who are often wrong about what is about to take place, are less than authentic?

## The skeptics

The skeptics, and there are a plethora of them "out there" ready to pounce at the first opportunity, will eagerly point out that if a psychic cannot be consistently correct with his forecasts of the future, it proves that all psychic phenomena is as believable as the tooth-fairy and the gnomes and elves who reside in the enchanted forest. They don't all necessarily imply that *all* psychics are charlatans or frauds intent on bilking the public for personal profit. Some will suggest that as well meaning as the psychics may be, they have no more access to the truth than random chance.

Isn't there an old saying—something about 100 monkeys at 100 typewriters that would eventually type *War and Peace* given enough time?

If we were to look past the Biblical and spiritual prophecies and a few of the more well-known psychic forecasts such as those penned by Nostradamus and Cayce, is there any proof that the future is actually preordained?

As we look at this question more closely, it appears that numerous indigenous cultures separated by great distances and large oceans possessed similar information or had analogous myths regarding events that were to occur in the future. Not only did they each have a familiar creation story describing the origin of their species but they had similar prophecies concerning the "last days."

## Incan warnings

The Incas in South America and the Hopis in what is now the American Southwest, for example, had both been warned about the "turtles" that would come from the sea and forever impact their culture. It would not be a far stretch of the imagination to visualize the Spanish conquistadors dressed in suits of armor being seen as fulfilling that warning.

Although they both spoke of tumultuous changes happening in the earth and the end of time as we know it, many of their prophecies are optimistic. They speak to a possible new golden age, an age of peace and emergence of a new human form.

## The legends of the Sioux Indians

The great Oglala Sioux holy man, Nicholas Black Elk, revealed messages from the Great Spirit warning mankind of the coming of both World War I and World War II, followed by a third world-shaking event recognized by a red cover or cloak ("Red" China?). Dawson No Horse, another Oglala seer, stated that as we moved into the 21st century, times would be very difficult. Not too many people could argue with that in light of the 9/11 tragedy.

Are we to assume that these spiritual messages foretell a time when all will be lost and mankind will be destroyed? The Sioux have a legend that comes from the constellation of stars commonly called Orion's belt. Known as the "Heart of the white buffalo," it states that a sacred maiden would return to help them when they were in trouble. When she left she turned into a black buffalo then a red buffalo, then a yellow buffalo and finally into a white buffalo before disappearing into the clouds. In August of 1994, a rare white buffalo was born in Wisconsin followed by two more in South Dakota several years later.

Black Elk later spoke of the thousand years of peace that is to follow what he called the third-world shaking, speculated by some to mean a war or violent earthquake. Interestingly, The Bible also speaks of the thousand years of peace following the Tribulation.

## The Hopi prophesies

The Hopi Native Americans have one of the better-known legends that they claim was delivered by the Great Spirit shortly after time began. It comes in the form of an oral tradition that has dutifully been passed down from generation to generation. They tell us that the Great Spirit divided the peoples of the earth into four groups and gave the "red man" the guardianship of the earth. They state that members of the "yellow race" were to be the keepers of the wind (breathing being a key technique to enlightenment according to many of the Eastern spiritual traditions). To the black men were given the guardianship of the water (the symbol of humbleness, patience and power). The white men were designated to be the guardians of the fire (the heart of any energy machine is a spark or fire with which to power it, to say nothing of the explosion of a nuclear weapon).

In addition the Hopi are said to possess stone tablets not unlike those the Bible states were given to Moses. The tablets have been dated to be between 10,000 and 50,000 years old and are kept at the Hopi Reservation in Arizona at the Four Corners Area on the Third Mesa. These, along with the ancient oral traditions speak of the things to come.

These legends and tablets also spoke of the warning signs leading up to the end of times. They told of the coming of the white man who would "strike their enemies with thunder" (guns?) and bring strange beasts with great long horns (cattle?) long before Columbus. They were warned that their land would be crossed by "snakes of iron" (trains?) running from east to west, "spinning wheels filled with voices" (covered wagons?) and a "giant spider web" covering the earth (power, Internet and telephone lines?). They were informed that prior to the last days the seas would turn black (oil spills?) and dwelling places would be created in the heavens (space stations?). All of these would come to pass, they were told, before the dawn of what they refer to as the *fifth world.*

However, the Hopi suggests, as do many other indigenous cultures, that all is not lost. They believe that the "Horny Toad Woman" will help them in the time of need, ensuring that people with good hearts and those who live in harmony with the earth will survive.

Where is a horny toad woman when you really need one?

When the numerous legends of these remotely located ancient societies are compared, many speak of the end of one age and beginning of another. The vast majority share similar warning signs and many speak of the survival of the righteous. Many have ancient petro-glyphs suggesting past interactions with alien visitors or "Star Brothers" and the eventual return to a distant star that is the origin of their race.

There are those who even suggest, such as Peter Lemesurier in his book, *The Great Pyramid Decoded* [21] that the Great Pyramid of Giza was *not* a royal tomb as the travel brochures would suggest, but a kind of time capsule, an "evolutionary blueprint for mankind." He suggests that by applying a measurement called the *pyramid inch* along the variances in the route of the buildings passages and chambers, one could not only map many of the cataclysmic events of the past five thousand years but predict the future through the fourth millennium A.D.

How did they know?

How did they come to know this information?

It is a well known fact that many indigenous cultures seemed to have had an advanced knowledge of the way the universe works while scientifically advanced Europe remained in the Dark Ages. Many of these primitive societies somehow understood the movement of the heavens and developed accurate calendars to predict the growing seasons and floods. Many have come to believe that they came from distant star systems. The Hopi believe they descended from the Pleiades Lyra, a ring nebula.

Did this same information come from an alien culture who possessed the technology to seed this planet as well as predict the future? Was the story of the Sioux Indian maiden who turned into a black buffalo on her way to Orion a description of some sort of interplanetary vehicle guided by those who shared future events? Were the flaming objects in the last chapter of the Biblical actually space vehicles piloted by those with advanced knowledge and able to predict the future? Are the indigenous shamans who have attained knowledge of specific herbs with healing properties advised by some sort of energy beings from other dimensions?

The undeniable fact is that they knew.

> Sometimes I lie awake at night, and I ask, 'Where have I gone wrong?' Then a voice says to me, 'This is going to take more than one night.—Charlie Brown, Peanuts

# 11

# It must be working—we are still here

Although history has provided us with a few of what some would consider as serious self fulfilling prophesies, most of the ones that come to the attention of the general public nowadays are of the more distressing or bizarre variety. These often appear in the super market tabloids, uttered by a few publicity-seeking no-names striving for their fifteen minutes of fame. For example, a few modern-day clairvoyants have prophesied cataclysmic earth changes that were to occur prior to the end of the 20th century. It was said that these would result from violent earthquakes that would cause much of the western United States to sink into the ocean. Some predicted that San Diego and Los Angeles would become islands and Colorado would inherit new beachfront property. Others thought that the poles would shift or that global warming would cause the ice caps to melt and the ocean levels to rise, flooding coastal cities throughout the world.

These events have not taken place—or at least not as this book went to press—and the jury is still out on the apocalyptic predictions that mankind still faces some sort of an end-of-the-world scenario. However, we seem to be doing our best to fulfill these prophecies when you consider some of our past government leaders apparent lack of interest in environmental issues or the fanatic self-proclaimed religious zealots who are bent on their evil brand of terrorism.

## The gospel according to the National Enquirer

On a lighter note, some of new millennium predictions headlined in such periodicals as the *National Enquirer* have been somewhat more off the wall or just down right wacky. Included in the pages of these gossip periodicals have been such earth-shattering revelations as Madonna giving birth to quintuplets, Roseanne shedding her clothes and conducting a TV talk show from a nudist colony and the discovery of an abandoned alien space station complete with the bodies of dead extraterrestrials.

It was left for us to speculate if some members of the alien crew are still alive with plush governmental jobs in Washington DC.

I suppose that Bob Thrift's prediction in UFOCUS Magazine [22] of the long awaited landing of an alien space ship on the White House lawn some years back was a bit tongue-in-cheek. He reported that it was to occur while Clinton was still president. Buddy, Clinton's dog was going to be the first to approach it and, as universal tradition would have it, he would be made the earth's ambassador to the Galactic Federation. Some even speculated that Buddy's first official move would be to have his human master neutered . . . but I don't believe that for a moment.

As a result of these bizarre and eccentric forecasts, most folks have no difficulty equivocating those who profess to be able to access true spiritual wisdom through higher consciousness with carnival crystal ball gazers and gypsy fortune-tellers. Mix in a few television images of Madam Somebody-or-other peering over a deck of tarot cards while advertising a 900 number and many would rate psychics only slightly above ambulance chasing lawyers and IRS agents.

## Can psychics read the future?

As we have seen, while a select few so-called psychics in the past may have correctly divined some events before they occurred, most today would agree that those who currently attempt to predict future events miss the mark. In spite of the many predictions of world-ending disasters, we are still here, aren't we?

First, it is clear that many so-called psychics are simply not credible. The psychic who quite seriously predicted that Hillary Clinton would be forced to publicly deny a secret agreement with the Ashtar Command perhaps needs to revaluate his hold on reality. The soothsayers who claim to attend weekly board meetings with aliens might be smoking some of that stuff that Clinton said he never inhaled.

Others merely state the obvious. The psychics who proudly take credit for events such as the stock market ups and downs, making some wealthy while others will lose money, are not necessarily terribly insightful. Those who have prophesied the yielding of our coastlines to the ocean don't have to be rocket scientists to realize that Mother Earth is only reacting to our abuse of her planet. It is not a stretch to connect the increase in the number of earthquakes to a reaction to our environmental insensitivity. If pollution leads to global warming as many believe, the eventual melting of the polar icecaps will cause the level of the ocean water to rise, leading to the eventual flooding of our coastal cities.

However, many of the more credible sages, seers and metaphysicians who do have an access to a higher consciousness often prefer to simply keep whatever insights into the future they might have to themselves. They don't require the same ego strokes sought by those whose credentials or track records are suspect.

The truth is that most credible psychic practitioners do not make public predictions of future events at all—and there is a reason for that.

If you asked most people what it is that psychics do they would respond that they predict the future. Many would associate the word psychic with fortunetellers, palm readers or carnival gypsies, whose placards outside their tent triumph their ability to access future events.

Ever met a rich psychic? If they knew what was going to happen, wouldn't they all have bought Microsoft or Yahoo at its lowest price and sold before its demise? When I first became aware if my gift, I headed to Reno to cash in on this sudden ability of mine to know things. I decided to go to the Roulette Wheel and predict whether the number called was red or black, as near as a 50/50 bet that I could find. It wasn't rocket science to determine it was not profitable when none of my first dozen or so bets were correct.

Actually, very few credible psychics are able predict future events for several specific and primary reasons. The quantum physicist will tell you that his study of the randomness but interconnectedness of quarks suggests that the future or, in fact, existence itself is only a *possibility* rather than a measurable predictable event.

The metaphysician would simply suggest that the future can be changed!

## Moral implications

There are, of course, those who attempt to gain insight into the future in order to manipulate it for a wide variety of reasons. Some dabble in the black arts or the occult for the express purpose of personally profiting from the outcome. It has been said that Hitler actively pursued objects thought to contain mystical power in order to control the future. On the other end of the spiritual spectrum, those from more benevolent groups, such as mystics, spiritual avatars and priests of the ancient mystery schools, might seek glimpses of the future for the express purpose of protecting the planet or mankind.

Philosophers and theologians have long questioned the ethical issues connected with the professed ability to foresee the future. Scientists have speculated that since we only use about 10% of our brain, perhaps we possess the latent ability to move beyond our five senses but simply have forgotten how. As we get caught up in the technical world and become increasingly dependent on the material aspects of life we tend to depend on weather men and financial gurus for forecasts.

The caveman had to depend on his finely tuned senses of what was about to happen simply to survive. The Bible trumpets the abilities of the ancient prophets who foretold pending disasters for the benefit of a specific group of people. The animal kingdom contains numerous species that appear to possess the ability to accurately anticipate early or severe winters. How about a mother who has had a bad "feeling" concerning her children and taken an action that later proved to be fortuitous?

The ability to connect with this source can be quite beneficial if used properly.

Misuse it, though, and you risk getting the attention of what one of my friends calls the fate guy.

> *Imagination is more important than knowledge* ... —*Albert Einstein*

# 12

## Altering the Future

So .... what happens when we mess with the "fate or karma guy?" Can we really change the future? Would we be gaining more power than we were intended to possess? Would this create more karma than would be resolved?

Richard Bach, the well-respected author of *Jonathon Livingston Seagull* and *One*, suggests that each time we "alter the future" we, in effect, create *two* separate experiences. One of us lives as if we had continued on the path originally set in motion, while another one of us moves forward to a different outcome on some other parallel level of consciousness. It is as if our individual awareness could simultaneously coexist in several realities at one time!

Does the future already exist?

When asked to address this question, Albert Einstein speculated that we would have to first look at the nature of time itself. He postulated that if the future can be observed, then it has to have already existed, suggesting that there is no such thing as *absolute* time. Instead, he proved in his *Theory of Relativity* that time differs based on the observation and motion of the observer. This can be illustrated by the now accepted scientific premise that an astronaut in a spaceship approaching the speed of light would age more slowly than one who has never left the planet.

Time is relative to the observer

And how about wrapping your mind around this one: Let's assume there are three spaceships, each traveling in the same direction, one directly behind another at great but equal distances apart and at a constant and equal velocity approaching the speed of light. If the captain in the center of the three ships were to send a message to both the ship in front of him and the one following at the exact same time, because they remain equal distances apart, and because light travels at a constant speed, we would easily agree that each would receive the message at the exact same time.

However, one could also argue, with equal authority, that because the space ship in front is pulling away from the position from which the signal was given but the ship following is rapidly approaching the point of origin, the trailing ship will intercept the signal prior to the lead ship as the signal had a shorter distance to travel.

Who is correct?

Guess what? They both are.

Here is another one: Assume you are in the back of a space ship, again moving very close to the speed of light. If you were to toss a ball 20 foot in the air and it were to take two seconds before it returned to your hand, the guy standing next to you could safely argue that he could easily follow the flight of the ball as it traveled 40 feet-20 feet up and 20 feet down—in 2 seconds.

However, if you somehow possessed x-ray vision when the space ship passed by, a third observer on earth could accurately contend that because the ball left your hand when the craft was over, say, the Empire State Building in New York City but landed as it was passing by the Statue of Liberty, it traveled a few *miles* in those same two seconds.

Einstein went on to surmise that because time is relative to the observer, there is no reason why the past, present *and* future could not be perceived in varying order. Would this suggest it *is* possible, in theory at least, to allow one to perceive the future *before* it occurs? Perhaps we could conclude that what we label as the future is just *one* of *many* possible outcomes.

## New Age events

New Age spiritualists will suggest that the interventions of worldwide spiritual events were a positive influence on the negative predictions of Nostradamus and Cayce and others. Some even contend that the astrological event known as the Harmonic Convergence in 1987 and the awakening of consciousness on January 11, 1992 known as the 11:11 (1/11/9+2) altered the disastrous world-wide apocalyptic course of what might have been. Who can really say otherwise? After all, the Bible informs us that when two or more come together in Jesus' name, powerful forces are often put into play.

Could it really be possible that the collective energy of what people desire or believe would actually change the outcome of a situation or event? An analogy here might be if everyone goes to a party with the same intention that it will be fun, the energy level is obviously set at a higher level than if the collective consensus of the party goers has predetermined it will be boring.

The consciousness of the collective whole in this example clearly dictates the experience (reality) of the event.

## Cracks in time

This understanding of Einstein's concept of the relativity of time led to the advent of the understanding of quantum mechanics that is embraced by a majority of the scientific community today. First noticing that particles are influenced by the fact that they are being observed, many in the scientific community would now agree that time is a notion that is not constant...or, as some have even postulated, literally doesn't exist at all!

Think about it. If you are driving an automobile and are aware you are about to be hit by another car, don't things seem to "slow down" for you. Yet, an observer would most likely confuse the facts because it "happened so fast?" When you "can't wait" for an event doesn't time literally "crawl by" but when you are having a wonderful time, time seems to "fly?"

When I jumped off a fifty-foot cliff into a pool of water alongside a beautiful waterfall in Hawaii, it seemed like "forever" until I finally entered the water. I recall dozens of individual thoughts and was fully aware of the hundreds of individual drops of water hanging out alongside me as they descended at same rate as my body. Yet, these who observed the event saw it as a mere few seconds and would have missed it if they blinked twice.

In the same vein, we can't say time is continuous and unbroken either. In Judaism, it is said that the Messiah will appear at the "end" of time. When the Christian Christ came, the "old" time ended and a "new" time began.

The Inca and Hopi prophesies speak of *pachacutis*, or "changes" in time, when the veil between the worlds becomes thin and the ordinary perceptions of time and space become blurred. The contend that their are places where *causay*, the Original Energy of Creation, seeps into our world to influences events that occurred in the past, thereby changing the outcome of the future.

There are legions in numerous ancient cultures that speak of sorcerers who have been said to have attempted to time journey through these cracks in time only to have had their luminous bodies often shredded or trapped in between worlds. Tibetan monks have told me of the existence of remains of their ancient brethren they have found trapped in the solid stone walls of their monasteries, perhaps while attempting to negate time in order to travel through a solid object. The room above the King's chamber in the Great Pyramid is said to be obtainable only by passing through solid stone, a feat requiring the alteration of both space and time.

## Faster than the speed of light

The great Danish physicist Niels Bohr, who often worked and shared ideas with Einstein, puts yet another spin to this time/space thing. He believed that subatomic particles travel so fast in time that he was able to "prove" that they are literally in several places at once. What he didn't understand was how if you were somehow able to pin one down by the act of measuring it, how it would be forced to choose one location over all the others?

Hugh Everett, his young physics grad student, took it to the next step. He concluded that since the motions and locations of these subatomic particles can never be accurately predicted, if you were somehow able to pinpoint and freeze one, it would be forced to split into multiple universes. Since the same particle would then be in two places at once, each particle would be required to seek its own separate future.

The irony was that the flower children of that same era did all of this by simply inhaling a bit of cannabis. I guess the old "tune in, turn on, drop out" theorem never made the scientific journals.

Want more? Just recently, researchers have challenged Einstein's theory even further. For nearly a century, physicists have believed that anything moving faster than the 186,828 miles per second or the speed of light would violate the most basic notion of physics. Anything moving faster would be like taking a sneak peak into the future.

However, Lijun Wang of the NEC researcher institute in Princeton, New Jersey, has reportedly produced light beams in the laboratory that have traveled faster than the normal speed of light, something heretofore thought to be impossible. In this experiment, a pulse of light was passed through a transparent chamber filled with cesium gas and was pushed to a speed 300 times faster than the normal speed of light. This is so fast, Wang reports, that the main part of the pulse exited the chamber even before it entered! This is as if someone on a sidewalk was to see an automobile accident well before the mishap occurred!

If this is true, could someone go back in time and kill our ancestors and negate our birth?

What we are talking about here is a preview of the future, although scientists are quick to point out that because light is a wave and has no mass, the above example of the accident could not really happen...or could it! Those who believe that we have been visited by alien space craft might point to this theory to explain how they are able to travel thousands of light years in relatively short "time periods."

Now if we were really adventuresome, we could expand this dialogue and argue the connection of alternate universes and worm holes. Einstein argued that objects with extremely large masses, better known as black holes, physically stretch and tear the fabric of space-time creating "alternate" time, thereby allowing for the theoretical potential of time travel.

More fodder for the UFOligests?

Then there is Steven Hawking's notion that this tear in the fabric of time would create what he labels "baby universes," and that would each would ultimately expand and grow, each forming its own separate self-contained branch of space-time. And then there is the notion of cosmic strings, the thin strands of energy millions of light-years long, and the theory of particle physics...

## Shaman physics

Follow all of this...? Me neither, but indigenous shamans have been doing this for years by melding their reality with the natural energy found all around us - the basic substance of creation.

Be clear that shamans and healers do not actually possess any magical power themselves; rather they have learned how access a different reality in order to utilize the natural energies in and of the earth. Throughout the ages, shamans have used simple techniques to alter their reality. It is well known that the sources of many of today's drugs are derivatives of roots or plants first discovered by the shamans while in an altered state. The ancient Mayans, for example, were well known for their knowledge of medicines found in plants. They were aware that everything in existence was part of the One. This philosophy extended to the belief and that the human body and the plants in the rainforests were interconnected and part of the same basic vibration. Their shamans seemed to possess the ability to read the auras of the both the patient and the plant, allowing them to match the need with the cure.

Ahhhh...the advanced wisdom of a primitive culture...!

## Can healers change the future?

Deepak Chopra, a proponent of the Ayurvedic approach to healing, explains this phenomenon in his books and lectures by suggesting that our bodies are like a 3-D projection or hologram of one's *current* state of mind. He contends that every thought is felt by everything else in existence and is therefore interconnected and is a equal part of a Larger Whole. Chopra suggests that by changing our thinking, we can alter the 50 trillion cells in our bodies into sharing new thoughts leading to an improved state of health. All it takes is intention and belief.

Most spiritual leaders, from indigenous tribal shaman to Eastern mystics, believe that we can change the "potential" course of future events. To believe that the future has been predetermined would suggest that we are puppets on some sort of long spiritual string.

Here is a practical exercise to try yourself. If you were to ask your higher guidance at bedtime just before entering the dream state how to best prepare to deal with a specific situation, you could be provided useful information allowing you to alter what might be one of many possible scenarios. Then pay attention, as the answers may come in a variety of forms. You may get a dream, get in touch with a feeling or even be the recipient of what you might perceive as a "coincidence" event leading you to a solution.

Remember: to expect that the outcome of every event is preordained gives away your power. To expect or create an improved outcome reclaims your ability to create a reality that is positive and purposeful.

## The future is one of many possibilities

Many modern-day mystics and shamans believe that the future is nothing more than a projection of what might happen if we don't get in the way of it. Cayce goes so far as to label current events as a "past condition," that is to say, the events of this dimension are simply a projection or reflection of what is being constructed at another higher level of consciousness. By intentionally paying attention to supernatural events such as our dreams, Cayce, and others, contend that we can tune into these higher levels and "see" what is being projected unless we choose to change it. A precognitive dream, one that suggests the future, is merely a glimpse of what may come into manifestation or one of *many* possible scenarios.

If you don't like it . . . don't buy it!

The concept of free will, which most spiritual teachings espouse, supports this contention. We are free to make whatever changes we wish, once we know that a change is desirable or necessary. By tuning into your higher consciousness such as your intuition, subtle feelings, and synchronistic events you can begin to be aware of what is in your best interest.

In a recent spiritual psychic reading, I advised a client to check the tires on his car. I did not see a pending accident; only provided information that could be considered or ignored completely. The recipient of the information had the free will to determine his own course of action.

Rather than being the victim, we can take charge of our own lives and create a reality that serves our higher knowing.

## Change the future

Often we alter the future without even knowing it. For example, a personal angel, spirit guide or spiritual intermediary might cause the phone to ring as you walk out the door thereby causing you to avoid a serious accident had you left on time. Although you might leave the house angry with the solicitor who may have delayed you, a higher power may have just saved your life.

You can take positive action to alter the outcome of your life. The methods are numerous. Where the Navajo shaman might invoke the ancestor spirits to intercede, the Shuar shaman in the Ecuadorian rain forest would simply re-dream the future. As the Eastern devotee may chant for clarity, the Western Christian might recite a prayer. In any case, by altering our belief system and intention we can shape-shift the future and avoid or change what some might have conceded as a preconceived outcome.

Do YOU have the power to change the events in your life?

The better question is . . . "Do you have the courage to do so?"

Let's look at some of the specifics on how . . .

*The Universe will reward you for taking risks on its behalf—Shakti Gawain*

# 13

# Connecting with your Spirit Guides

So . . . how do we safely tune in to this inner knowing or psychic input?

In the old days, sorcerers and wizards claimed to have sole domination over this collective realm of esoteric omnipotence for purposes of power or control. Some made alliances with the devil or negative or black forces and gave little or no concern to destroying all who might stand in their way. Others turned to God or the White Light to guide the planet away from its historically documented movement toward self-destruction. Others simply went within, in order to *submit* to any available mystical authority with the goal of reaching the subliminal glow of the Creative Force or nirvana.

Most did it in the name of religion.

The means to perceive this recondite wisdom is available to all who seek it. It can vary with each individual and can be discerned in many ways. Many times it will *first* occur as a warning, a "feeling" or a sudden "knowing." It may be a voice that alerts us to a potential problem or negative situation. It might come in the form of a dream or a sudden glimpse of a scene across the room that reminds you of something you must consider.

In whatever form it takes it will provide us with clarity when we need it the most. If we were to pay attention, we could sidestep an avoidable problem or learn an intended lesson. Who knows? We might even resolve some negative, past-life karma.

## Unexpected messages

These messages most often begin in ways that are not only unexpected but manifest through a sense we have largely ignored. An acquaintance of mine was driving along an unfamiliar freeway when he suddenly experienced a terrible pain in his chest. The discomfort was so severe that his wife insisted that he pull his car to the side of the road, fearful that he might be experiencing a heart attack. Then, thirty seconds later, it dissipated, just as suddenly as it had begun.

Taking no chances, his wife slid into the driver's seat and pulled back onto the roadway anxious to find a hospital or medical clinic. Several moments after resuming their journey, they came upon a terrible automobile accident just ahead of them on the freeway. A truck, loaded with scaffolding was stopped in the center lane with what appeared part of its load scattered about the adjacent lanes and with a car accordioned up against the back tailgate, its windshield smashed and debris all over the hood.

Impatient to get her husband to medical attention she pulled off onto the shoulder of the road, hoping to avoid the delay and make it to the next exit. As she pulled alongside the calamity a sudden chill swept over the two of them. The very truck they had been following seconds before the onslaught of her husband's sudden pain had lost a good portion of its load of scaffolding and a sharp pipe-like object was sticking through the windshield, impaling the driver through the chest!

Had it not been for the psychic warning, the precognitive discomfort he received from an astral level, this ride could have been physically life-threatening!

## Recognizing the communication

First, we must learn how to recognize these warnings or communications from this higher source. It might be said that this unseen non-physical essence creates something similar to an energy "wave," much as a change in humidity or sudden wind indicates an approaching storm.

Anyone who has confronted an unfriendly ghost or had a scary encounter with a negative essence often mentions a cold draft, bumping or a dull sound. They might speak of an eerie feeling when describing what they "felt."

On the other hand, the presence of a positive force is generally characterized as a pleasant sensation. A soft light is often associated with a visitation from an angel. Tinkling chimes or soft bells have been linked to a spiritual encounter. Religious experiences are often accompanied by an overwhelming feeling of peace or protection.

Often these experiences will appear in the form of a dream, hallucination or even a synchronistical occurrence. Since these messengers are considered to be non-physical, it is not unusual to have them take the form of what many consider to be the "non-reality" of the shaman's dreamtime.

## Opening to the experience

OK ... now that we know how to recognize the signs, what do we do and how can we draw this metaphysical wavelength to us?

The simplest answer is simply to open yourself to the experience! We are so accustomed to tuning out the multitude of extemporaneous perceptions that bombard us daily that we often overlook information that is right in front of us.

To illustrate this point, as you read this book, be cognizant of the variety of sounds swirling around you. Close your eyes and become aware of the vibrations of the predominant colors in your immediate vicinity. Become aware of the many sensations your body continually records but which often go unnoticed by you. Tune into the feel of your clothing on your skin or the rhythm of your breathing.

Interesting what you might notice when you direct your attention to it.

Once you get in touch with this subtle level of awareness, heed the abstruse signals being presented by your inner personal "guidance. Ask yourself, "if there were a message here what would it be?" You might "imagine" a potential new scenario or "remember" a past experience which might apply to your inquiry—all the while unlocking the door to a higher truth.

Then just be with it, observing what happens.

In other words, go with the flow.

Most often this begins as a very subtle perception, much like knowing that something is out of place or that someone is staring at you. You might "accidentally" encounter a friend who "coincidentally" imparts some useful information or you overhear an informative conversation, which relates to your specific situation.

## Getting answers

Then, as you begin to successfully tune in to this inherent ability on a regular basis, you may request answers to specific questions regarding our everyday life. For example, if you desire a new career in which to fulfill your creative talents, ask your guidance if the timing is right. If it is, you may receive conformation by receiving an advertising circular in the mail informing you of a desirable job opportunity. If you wish to attract a relationship, you might run into an old friend who invites you to a party where your potential mate awaits your notice.

If you are looking for input regarding a decision, begin the question with, "Is it in my best interest . . ." If it involves another person ask only for information as doing otherwise might impact you. If you are requesting guidance regarding an activity, request that you be moved forward only if it is in your highest and best interest or if there is a lesson to be learned in the process. Work with a few of the tools that are readily available at metaphysical bookstores such as Angel Cards, Runes, the I Ching and a pendulum to mention just a few.

Once you have made the initial connection with your higher self or guides, you can begin to do it instantaneously, much as you might turn to a co-worker for the answer to a problem. Begin by asking a question of them before you fall asleep and see how you feel about the issue in the morning. Then begin to dialogue with them in your meditation, whether by way of a formal ceremony in a sacred space or in a less formal setting, such as watching a tropical sunset or a walk along a quiet beach. Lie on your back and observe the patterns in the clouds drift by in the afternoon sky. Perhaps you will hear the answer in a casual discussion with a friend or you will "by chance" overhear a conversation that provides the resolution to your problem.

Sychronicity is still alive and well this side of Oz.

## Gaining confidence

As your guidance becomes more active, you will gain additional confidence and begin to rely on the process in the more routine portions of your day-to-day life. You will begin to notice situations that had previously escaped your attention and to become aware of options you may not have formerly considered.

Two notes of caution though. First, only ask for guidance and direction that is positive. Never request spiritual assistance that might be harmful to someone else. Inquiring how to gain something at the expense of others is not a proper use of this conduit. Instead, seek direction regarding the discovery of your higher potential.

Secondly, when you dwell on something negative, your guidance will only assume that you are expecting the negativity and they just may attempt to comply with your wishes. For example, if you feel you have a 50/50 chance of doing something incorrectly because you always seem to do it wrong, your guides will only assume you want to fail again or you would not be dwelling on it. When you tell a friend that you will probably mess it up because you got it wrong the last three times, your guides may think you are trying to go for a record fourth time! "Why else would you be thinking that," they would assume, "if you did not want (create) some more?"

## Visualization

Visualize only the higher spiritual source or philosophy with which you feel comfortable. Surround yourself with the white light of pure thought, or of God, or any positive icon which has meaning to you. To make a pact with the devil is to bring on a force you may not wish to serve. The law of karma suggests that all that occurs begins with our own thought and is reinforced by our actions.

To have clear intentions and a clear heart is a wise use of the power.

This is not to suggest that this procedure should be a substitute for your current spiritual devotion to however you personally perceive the Creative Source. It is not to circumvent your religious convictions or to shortcut your way to personal riches or ego-based success. Not at all... instead it is simply meant to provide access to the same intuitive awareness on which the prehistoric caveman relied to warn of unseen potential dangers. It is what guided the indigenous natives to discover the medicinal values of specific roots and herbs.

It is probably what led Columbus to the New World and what's-his-name to the discovery of penicillin...

It's what provided my wife Shirl the message to sing *Kumbaya* in a dark moment.

> *A positive attitude may not solve all your problems, but it will annoy enough people to make it worth the effort"*—Herm Albright

## 14

# Escaping With Our Lives

Being able to access this higher awareness literally saved our lives.

My wife Shirl and I have been on our spiritual journey for some time, observing and learning from indigenous shamans in their natural habitat. Our travels have taken us to many remote portions of the world, hooking up with anyone who could provide an opportunity to meet with authentic healers and seers. On one such sojourn, we found ourselves in the region of the lower Omo River in the most southern- and most remote-portion of Ethiopia, visiting areas that see few foreign visitors.

We had made the long, hot trek to visit the Merci tribe and we had set up camp late in the evening alongside the river while pretending to ignore the loud cracks of rifle fire as the natives hunted crocodiles. Quickly jumping into our makeshift tents protected only by a thin band of rented canvas, we bravely hoped that if we couldn't see what was out there, the local predators would not know that there were new arrivals on their food chain.

We woke the next morning to the smell of coffee and the curious, searching eyes of a few women from the nearby village who had come to examine our encampment at the first light.

## Indigenous living art

Because symbolism is extremely important in their culture, they each proudly displayed their tribal status on their bodies. The women wore painted decorations but accented them with major piercings of their facial orifices such as lips, chins, noses and ears. It would not be unusual to observe an opening in a woman's ear lobe larger than a half dollar or a piece of body decoration attached to the face by way of a nail driven through their skin. The women all wore lip plates 4 inches in diameter and ½ inch thick that had been placed in a slit in their lower lip.

The men all looked like warriors. They proudly displayed large white circular designs painted around their eyes, noses and mouths along with numerous small repetitive circular patterns etched deeply into their jet black chests, stomachs and legs. Some wore unique scarves or animal hides about their heads or shoulders.

These people are incredible living works of art, with each subtle embellishment a notation of specific social status, beauty and bravery. While we were anxious to experience their music, drumming, dancing and stories that spoke to their cultural heritage, it was clear that their bodies are their resumes, expressing their personal accomplishments and social ranking in the tribe. From the distinctively shaped topknots on shaved heads to the heavy metal jewelry, beads and feathers, both genders would be readily noticeable stateside, even in San Francisco.

# The Nature Of Reality . . .

The spiritual leader of this tribe was undisputedly the shaman, whose ethereal guidance and ability to heal was well respected. We were anxious to meet him as we had been told that he had complete freedom to set the spiritual agenda of his village. His exact job description was somewhat arguable but it included treating the sick, pacifying disruptive earth spirits and officiating in the ceremonies marking the passage of the children into adulthood.

However, unlike the ministers in our culture, this shaman is not forced to sponsor bingo games, drawings and rummage sales in order to compete with a priest-magician of another denomination down the block.

## Running into trouble

By the time we had collected together for breakfast, a dozen or so of the Merci women had gathered at the edge of our encampment, knowing we would be most likely be easy marks to purchase some of the native wear. The women always seem to approach us first, a reflection of the African women's more assertive role in their culture. While the Merci had seen few outsiders, they had clearly learned one basic lesson about foreigners—they were potential customers for their authentic hand-made goods.

It was clearly a seller's market.

It was a classic Kodak moment and Shirl wasted no time lining up a group of six women and had negotiated a price to have her photograph taken with them. While she went about choreographing the team photo, a few men happened by and I could sense they were less eager to be hospitable than their female counterparts.

Shirl motioned for me to take the photo. I grabbed her camera and hastily clicked the shutter. As Shirley paid each of them the previously stipulated rate of several burr notes, one of the Merci women suddenly grabbed at Shirl's fanny pack and made an unscheduled withdrawal from her depository of funds. Another threw the burr notes she had been given to the ground and began to shriek in a voice suggesting that she was less than completely pleased with the amount of the payment she had been presented.

Instinctively reacting to the struggle, I stepped into the fray to grab back the purse. At that, the more subtle mannerisms of the men began to quickly transform into a more aggressive and confrontational behavior. The previously negotiated prices for their trinkets and photographs suddenly became null and void as the Merci men whose numbers seemed to be increasing, began to physically intimidate our group with their laughing and jeering.

As their attitude became more belligerent, our little group of travelers instinctively began to retreat inward toward the center of our camp. The campfire was still burning the remnants of the partially eaten breakfasts created by our cook from the rapidly depleting canned supplies carried in the vehicle. As the shouting of the Merci women and the threatening taunting from the men increased, our guide and driver began to hurriedly break camp, recklessly throwing the tents and cooking utensils in the back of the vehicle without much regard to order.

It was then that I became aware of the unmistakable click of a "safety" being released on a rifle carried by a young warrior who towered over me and whose facial expression, inches from mine, suggested that his grip on reason and stability might be somewhat in doubt.

Several of the women in our group began to cry while several others exhibited an unmistakable look of panic. The more the Merci pressed forward, the more tension radiated throughout the camp.

I flashed on a collage of vintage Western movies: Canestoga Wagons drawn in a tight circle while a group of nervously circling Indians waited for an opening to attack the intruding and uninvited white settlers they suddenly discovered in their midst.

It was truly an intense moment. We were miles away from a pay telephone and a quick scan of the horizon suggested that the US Calvary would not miraculously appear to save *this* wagon train.

## Spirit guide intervention

Knowing that these fierce appearing warriors could probably blow us away and not miss a meal, I really considered that we would not need our return airline ticket home. I glanced over to Shirl hoping to comfort her and I saw her staring to the heavens as she does when she receives inspiration from her spirit guides.

All of a sudden her face lit up with a huge smile and, turning to the woman who had been crying, she whispered something in her ear. The woman hesitated, stopped her sobbing and leaned towards the woman next to her, repeating the message. She in turn passed it on to the next.

Shirl glanced at me and with the look every married man recognizes as, "Trust me and follow my lead," began to sing.

"*Kumbaya my Lord, Kumbaya. My Lord, Kumbaya.*"

Several others, instinctively, picked up the words and soon our entire circle joined in and sang the song we all probably first learned on a Scout outing, Bible camp or a beach party just as the marshmallows melted on the end of the sticks held too close to the campfire.

"*Kumbaya my Lord . . .*"

As I glanced around at the local tribesmen and women, their painted faces reflecting a culture I did not understand, I began to perceive a small shift in energy.

"*My Lord, kumbaya . . .*"

An energy shift

And then he appeared. The shaman we had come to meet, calmly walked over to Shirl and removed one of the many beaded necklaces that he proudly wore and placed it around her neck.

With that, several of the Merci women began to smile a bit; several others began to sway to the music while an unspoken directive instructed us to join hands as we began another verse with a little more vigor. The volume of our singing seemed to increase in proportion to our returning confidence and we quickly became one with the song.

Gradually, the raw emotion resulting from the villager's inherent suspicion and resistance to anything strange or foreign began to dissipate with each additional chorus of the music.

When you stop to think about it, it is not surprising that the initial response of the villagers' was similar to the old classic science fiction movies of the 1950's when humans first encountered strange visitors from outer space. It wouldn't take long until the army generals would show up with tanks and guns, shooting at the uninvited invaders. I guess our species is no different than the others on earth, conditioned to be threatened by anyone who appears to be different from us.

## A common connection

As the suspicion began to dissipate, the seeds of a gradual acceptance of the differences between our two incongruous cultures sharing the same tiny planet began to emerge. The introduction of a universal common language—music—was the catalyst. Although the Merci people obviously did not know the meaning of the words, the soothing sounds of the melody are recognizable cross culturally.

Another of the men approached Shirl and offered her his arm bracelet and showed her how it moved as he danced and swayed his body. Uncertain if this was a friendly gesture or the beginning of an unusual mating ritual, I stood close by as if to say that she was MY woman.

With the third chorus of *kumbaya* near completion and the tension diffused for the moment, an unspoken command suggested that we slowly grab our stuff and ease ourselves towards the vehicle. With very little discussion as to whose turn it was to ride where, we quickly jumped in, secure within the safety of a product of our familiar culture.

It did not take a rocket scientist to determine that it was time to leave.

> History is the version of the past that people have decided to agree upon . . .
> —Napoleon Bonaparte

# 15

# Ancient tools—historical perspective

Many people, unaware of their natural psychic-intuitive ability to gain their own answers, will instead turn to the council of mediums to contact the departed or psychics to forecast their future. Most first-timers who come to me seeking a psychic reading expect me to tell them what is going to happen. Will I be successful in business? When will I find my soul mate? What will I be doing or where will I be living five years from now?

## Fortune tellers

Probably the most common image of the psychic is that of the *scryer*, or crystal gazer. Most commonly associated with the wondering gypsies of eastern Europe, mediums are often portrayed as being in some sort of trancelike, gazing into a crystal ball, precious stone or other reflective surface. Some claim to access their divination powers from staring into tea leaves, thumbnails, blood or ink.

Remember the story of Snow White? The wicked witch consulted her magic reflective mirror to provide the information she was seeking.

Another common symbol of the "fortuneteller" is the palmist. This medium doesn't see the future as much as he or she determines "likely trends" or probable future. The palms are said to develop their characteristic lines and patterns and bumps or mounds from the time of birth. This art can be traced back to the ancient writing of scribes in India and China over 3,000 years ago.

Aristotle attributed the origins of palmistry to ancient Egypt. Nevill Drury and Gregory Tillett in their book, *The Occult* [23], suggest that "humans were linked with the Cosmos and an analysis of human nature (revealed in the hands) revealed the wider universe." They further point out that some modern psychologists have even correlated the lines on the hands with certain cases of mental disorders and personality characteristics. While not predicting the future, it might provide a means of alerting one to future possibilities.

## Scientific proof

Does any of this have any scientific proof? *Time Magazine* [24] reports on a new study that makes a correlation between the length of the index and ring-finger and the amount of testosterone people were exposed to in the womb. Dr. Marc Breedlove, a Berkeley, California psychologist who has been studying if there are anatomical clues that might suggest sexual preference or orientation, reports that lesbians tend to have substantially shorter index fingers than their straight counterparts. However, his study also shows, that really short index fingers on men don't mean they're gay or straight, but that they probably have lots of older brothers.

*Time* goes on to report that a similar study at Rutgers University found a considerable overlap between gay and straight women, but according to yet other recent studies, "women with long index fingers are more fertile." Moreover, "men with long ring fingers tend to be better soccer players and musicians, as well as more depressed and virile."

Scientific proof or superstitious poppycock, belief systems do not pass the test of time unless there is some merit to the process. When I first began to develop as a psychic, I would rely on the palms to provide "clues" which I would then expand upon intuitively. One hand would tell me what the individual came into this life to do or resolve and the other would suggest the present direction one was going. From this, the *probable* future could be ascertained.

However, the world-view professed by both the modern and ancient shaman would suggest that our future has *not* been predetermined; instead, we each have free will. We each have the ability to fulfill our karmic destiny. By seeking these same spiritual forces used by the shaman, we can access ancient understanding, which has been all but forgotten, in our hectic, fast-paced world.

Instead of asking spirit what will be, how about requesting guidance about what is . . . or simply how to change what you don't like?

Psychic tools

As previously mentioned, many metaphysical adventurers will search for their own answers by the use of other relatively popular and widely available products that can be readily found in numerous metaphysical or occult bookstores. Many will attest to the fact than when used properly, they can provide useful information regarding a suggested course of action to follow.

Of course, there were many other less well-known tools used in ancient days. Those who lived on the land utilized items that were commonly available. Alectryomancy, for example, was a common practice in farming communities. The practitioner would display the letters of the alphabet on the ground and, after placing a grain of wheat on each, note the order in which an animal would eat the wheat as a means of obtaining guidance for the problem at hand.

Those who worked the land in the British Isles in the days of the construction of Stonehenge were great believers in Geomancy, the observation of patterns in the earth. The position of large boulders, trees or mountain ranges or even the manner in which the rivers flowed would dictate the best location for the construction of a sacred site. (This of course was not to be confused with *Gyromancy*, which linguists will tell you is the practice of walking around in a circle until one falls and then drawing a conclusion from the direction and position assumed by the fallen body.)

## Sacred energy

Try it yourself. Once you select a sacred site, such as a circle of trees or boulders, walk around the inner core of the circle until you determine the exact center. Your center will probably differ from others but it's *your* center . . . stay with *your* feelings. Then close your eyes and "feel" the center as if you were in a large round theatre and you had to locate the exact middle point. Allow your spirit guides to nudge you as you make the minute adjustments. Then pose your question and listen for the response.

If you fall over you have selected the wrong process.

Oh . . . and don't do it unless you are prepared to hear the answer!

The ancient Chinese, for example, would not construct a structure until they first consulted the local Feng Shui practitioner, who would advise them of the proper design and placement for the greatest harmony of the inhabitants with the existing elements of the earth.

Deep forest peoples might adhere to some form of *Belomancy* to determine a specific location. It was not uncommon to have the shaman shoot an arrow into the air and have the projectile select the best location for a new village.

Even modern worshipers have been known to use a form of this selection process. Someone seeking answers might open a sacred text (such as the Bible or Koran) at a random location in search of an answer, trusting the selected sentence or paragraph to resolve a problem or offer advice. The ancients called this process the art of *Stichomancy*.

Charms and amulets

Many uses of physical objects also date back to Medieval times. Talismans or amulets, reflecting the tradition of the Hebrew Qabbalah, were often created for those who wished to influence an outcome or event. Since it was widely held that all things are related to one another through a series of correspondences, by evoking the mystical power of mystical symbols, the one believing in the power is said to be able to create a favorable outcome.

For example, if you wished to affect matters of love or partnerships, you might commission a charm representing the planet Venus. Those who believe in astrology have long considered that the major planets in our solar system have a direct influence on human behavior. The craftsman's creation would embody the specific metal, numbers or symbols associated with the planet in order to evoke its power.

If these physical amulets were not helpful, one might seek the verbal charms or spells dispensed by the alchemist, sorcerer, or high priestesses proficient in magic. It has been said that such historical personalities as Abraham, King Solomon and Pope Honorius III believed in and wrote about these mysterious powers of the universe.

Conversely, because the Inca medicine man believed that death grows within us from the moment of birth until it eventually consumes our life force, they would use a physical object to withdraw this anxiety into a physical object. The shamans would often breath their fear of death into their sacred stones, or huacus, and then discard them into a deep pool of water thereby shedding death into what they considered the life source.

## Rituals and magic

The Egyptians detailed the use of mysterious spoken verbal forces in *The Book Of The Dead*. Included were a combination of spells, incantations and rituals, all for the purpose of assuring the safe passage of the spirit of their dead king to the netherworld. This information was thought to be helpful if not necessary to assist the royal family along the route to eternal life. Much of the information would be spoken aloud by the priest (and presumably the soul of the departed) with proper pronunciation and specific motions and intonation. These beliefs, used as far back as the third century BC, were probably the single greatest influence in the rituals and spells of the civilizations which were to follow.

The ancient Masonic Order, The Rosicrucians and Knights Templars of old based much of their ceremonies on the use of this ritual magic. The Hopi Indians of New Mexico and Arizona continue to petition the earth spirits they call kachinas, or cloud spirits, to assist their way of life by providing rain and promoting a bountiful harvest.

Of course, one had to be careful not to employ practitioners of *black* magic. The distinction between white and black magic seemed to be in the magician's intent as well as the source of his or her supernatural powers. The black magician was said to bridge the gap between the living and the dead. English author Christopher Marlowe wrote a famous play about Johann Faust, a little-known German magician who was believed to have obtained his powers from the powers of both good and evil. French historian Jules Garinet wrote extensively about the misuse of this power by medieval French monks who would invert positive Christian rituals into devil-worship in the dark of night.

However, many cultures believed in the "magic" of a subtler kind. Synchronicity, the occurrence of simultaneous events related to one another, seems to have a magic of its own. These occurrences, such as what some people might perceive as a chance meeting of a friend or overhearing information, often led to the resolution of an issue or pressing concern.

Are these events merely coincidences or, perhaps, the result of an over-stimulated imagination? Maybe . . . but the shamans from a variety of cultures would suggest that this information, regardless of the form in which it occurs, is always readily available to each of us. All it takes for it to manifest is a need to know. With intention, commitment and rightful purpose, it becomes more readily accessible.

Oh yeah ... and a substantial belief that it is possible ... !

> *It is not in the stars to hold our destiny but in ourselves—William Shakespeare*

# 16

# There are many paths

There are probably as many paths to attaining higher consciousness as there are disciplines; each authentic in its own right. However, before we can select our specific path, we need to choose our direction. To do this, we need to first understand our relationship with the Creator and determine whether we perceive Him as a separate, powerful and sometimes vengeful God who demands full devotion from his subjects, or an omnipresent and benevolent energy, expressing Itself in all of life.

Those who might take the former view generally believe that the primary purpose of our brief experience in physical form is to seek a spiritual reward upon its completion, only if a judging God deems us worthy. Some ancient societies went so far as to conduct human sacrifices to pacify the ego of their deity or to construct large edifices as a testimony to His authority and supremacy.

## The Nature Of Reality...

Why wait?

Others who see the expression of the Creator consciousness in each one of us feel that there is no need to wait for the Day of Judgment to attain this higher state of awareness; it is available here and now. By understanding that we are an expression or extension of this Divine Spirit, we can experience a state of union with our higher self now and fully claim our role in the Creator's dream.

There are numerous spiritual and religious organizations worldwide that provide their flock with the means of "getting there;" each with its own doctrine and scripture to document its authenticity. However, in order to avoid the complexities and controversy of attempting to compare the merits of one with another, let's look beyond the religious dogma and consider a concept that allows us to access higher consciousness by simply quieting the fluctuations of the mind.

This viewpoint is expressed in many forms and doctrines and is recognizable in some of the New Age or Eastern traditions such as the Martial Arts and Yoga. These are not the only available methods, of course, but by examining a few of their precepts, we can garner some basic techniques that can be used to achieve higher understanding. The concepts are quite basic: they provide us methods to overcome the impurities of the mind-body caused by the imbalances or conditionings of physical form. Once accomplished, the reward is a clear understanding of oneself—a primary step to full awareness.

Going within

Yoga practitioners follow specific guidelines not unlike the commandments or tenets of most major religions. Ashtanga yoga practitioners, for example, seek to follow a course they describe as eight limbs or principles: [25]

> Yamas: Universal ethical principles and restraints for day-to-day life
> Niyamas: Authentic spiritual, personal and moral practices
> Asanas: Physical postures that connect body, mind and spirit
> Pranayama: Yoga breathing techniques to provide balance and harmony
> Pratyahara: Control of the senses in order to connect to Pure Essence
> Dharana: Concentration of the mind to eliminate distractions
> Dhyana: Meditation or deep prayer to listen to what has always been there
> Samadhi: Transcendence or absorption into the Infinite Mind

Six steps to non-attachment

In Hatha Yoga, there are six *Tapas* or disciplines one must follow in order to achieve the desired non-attachment state of *Vairaagya*. Let's examine these yoga concepts using practical terms with which we can all relate:

> 1. *Presence*—remaining in the present moment. Time is a concept that we use to mark our journey in physical form. From a spiritual point of view, time does not exist, since everything is truly just a moment of now. If God "always was," and is omnipresent, and if we are an aspect of this Creator Force,

then it follows that time is an earthbound concept that can be circumvented when reaching a higher consciousness.

2. *Persistence*—making a commitment and staying with the belief that all things are possible. This can relate to everything from a yoga pose to developing the patience and determination to attain spiritual awareness and the ultimate connection with the All That Is that follows.

3. *Repetition*—Locking on to a belief system and walking your talk. This requires the willingness to repeat things over and over until they become second nature and become your truth. Remember, when you change your belief system you create a *new* reality.

4. *Restraint*—Perhaps one of the toughest disciplines, it requires eliminating the old ways of being that are spiritually distracting or destructive. This requires the awareness to both recognize and avoid the old destructive patterns that no longer serve your highest and best interest.

5. *Release*—In Yoga terms this refers to letting go of the resistance to a pose; however, in everyday language it might refer to whatever is in the way of the desired spiritual practice. Often it means letting go of control, the left-brain, logical part of each of us that operates entirely from past experiences and easing into what feels right.

6. *Risk*—The willingness to explore new territory and trusting that the higher self will guide you to where you need to go. By hanging onto old patterns we all become locked into physical and emotional limitations that stymie our spiritual growth.

## Ten ways to higher consciousness

Now that we are clear on the procedure to follow, we need practical methods to follow—a vehicle to get us where we want to go. How do we know which path to take? How do we scale the mountain of consciousness?

Again, there are as many ways to achieve this state of mind, as there are disciplines:

1. From a purely Christian point of view, Jesus provided the answer in the very first commandment when he said, "Thou shall love thy God with all thy heart, and with all thy soul and with all thy mind, and with all thy strength." By being aware of the grace of God and knowing that He is love, we begin to recognize that we are an individual expression of this Spirit, and, as such, need only to turn inward to find what we are looking for. Explore the feelings of forgiveness and gratitude and notice a new way of being.

Rather simple, isn't it?

2. Meditation is a useful method and something with which we all are familiar. While it shares some similarities with prayer, meditation is less the act of asking and more the art of listening. To accomplish this, set aside a time or space that is sacred and create a ceremony around your intent to receive direction from a higher guidance or consciousness. This need not be confined to sitting cross-legged in a yoga pose—you can achieve this by hiking to the top of a spiritual mountain, becoming one with a circle of trees, watching the surf pound the rocks

along a rugged coast line or even walking a beach sipping a glass of wine as you watch the sunset with someone special.

Expect to receive the information you wish to hear!

3. Some who profess to recognize and communicate with the natural earth energies might have you call on the crones or sacred goddesses of history who are said to nourish and protect the earth. These energies go by many names such as Gaia from Greece, Vesta from Rome, Isis from Egypt, Benton from Japan and Ala from Africa. Still others would include Spider Woman from the Native American culture, Baba Yaga from Mother Russia, Kwan Yin from ancient China, Rhiannon from the Druid culture of Wales and, of course, the Blessed Virgin Mary, Mother of Jesus.

There are many ways to "get there." Why not call and see who shows up?

4. Indigenous shamans from the remote rainforests of the world call on their power animals, personal spirit guides or ancestor spirits to reach out to what some call the Upper World. They perceive these energy forms much as the Catholic Church might see a guardian angel. Try it yourself. Before you drift off to sleep, ask your higher self to make the spiritual connection for you. You may wake with a dream or perhaps receive some information weeks later inviting you to explore a new way of being. You can also program yourself to wake up in the morning with a word or phrase that will suggest a course of action to follow.

How can you expect to get answers if you don't ask the questions?

5. Avail yourself of some of the many ancient tools that are accessible through metaphysical bookstores. The pendulum, I Ching, Angel cards or runes are only a few aids that may open the channels of communication in order to provide direction on your journey. Pay attention to the information that comes your way such as classes to open to your psychic awareness or in how to understand your dreams. Go to the metaphysical or spiritual portion of a bookstore and notice what seems to "fall into your hands."

Delight in your progress. Remember, nothing ventured, nothing gained.

6. Get in touch with your natural intuitive or psychic nature. Begin to pay attention to when you knew something was about to occur before it happened. Notice how many times you almost said, "I knew you were going to say that" or the feeling you had when you knew the phone was about to ring. Allow the inner voice to provide you with an increased sense of knowing and recognize the patterns of successful communication so that you might begin to generate your own contact.

Of course, remember: they used to burn witches at the stake for doing less.

7. Become aware of how simply tuning into your own body can bring you to an elevated state of awareness. If you can appreciate how music can change your mood, imagine what listening to chanting monks in Tibet might do to your state of being. If you understand how pausing and taking a deep breath can bring about calmness, imagine what a week of holotropic breathing might do for your awareness. If you feel free when dancing, imagine what a "whirling dervish" must experience when letting the body have total freedom

And the best part? Everyone has the built-in equipment to do it.

8. A shaman in the Brazilian rainforest, dressed in a loin cloth with feathers in his hair summed it up this way: First, *manifest what you want*. As has been previously stated, we each have the power to create what we want or need. Call it the power of positive thinking or affirmations if you wish but discard the negative way of thinking. Since all things are energy, to worry about something is to bring it into being in some form. If you believe hard enough that something is possible—with great intensity and a belief it can happen—you begin to realize that it exists. Then, once you are clear on what you want, the next step is *to know that you already possess it*. You cannot have something until you have the capacity to already possess it. Then, let go of all the reasons it couldn't possibly happen.

Dorothy had to believe the ruby slippers had the power before they worked!

9. Travel to the rain forest of South America, retreat to the spiritual mountains of Tibet or explore the tribal villages in the American Southwest and seek the services of a reputable holy man or shaman. Shamans tune into the spirit energy of the earth. Said to be able to *shapeshift*, they are able to move into the upper, middle and lower worlds and from the past time the future. It is from this virtual state of what they call *dreamtime*, where the past and future are nothing more than the 'moment of now,' that they are able to dream things or events into existence.

Didn't Jesus say seek and you shall receive? You don't have to be a shaman to try it.

10. Astral projection or remote viewing has been well documented by researchers as a legitimate perception that one is traveling to a familiar location while still remaining fully conscious of their body space. Accessible through both the sleep and waking state, many people have accurately reported on the activities of "targets" miles from their location in real time. Both Russian and American governments have used psychics to spy on their adversaries. Arrange to meet a friend in the dream state and compare notes upon waking.

There are some implied rules here such as: the girls' locker room is out of bounds!

We are in the bonus round now—want to really go out on a limb?

Want to live a bit more on the edge? While the above methods are somewhat tame by comparison, the following are just a few more extreme methods that have reportedly shifted earth-bound awareness to an alternate state of consciousness. Just like the disclaimer on TV that states "Do not try these at home: these stunts are done by professionals," I advise you to research each method carefully and talk to those who have done it before attempting to do any of them yourself.

An "out-of-body" experience is similar to astral projection except that one feels that he or she is observing his or her surroundings from a location outside the body. Robert Monroe, one of the early pioneers reporting OBE phenomena describes a sensation of a separate "second self," or astral consciousness, that observes and is connected to the physical body by a silvery elastic cord. The problem is that legend says that if the cord is broken the journeyer may not be able to return to his body!

There are some occult tools that I recommend you avoid such as the Ouiji board. Although you will often see this in game form, its true purpose is to summon spirits from the other side. The problem is, you don't always have control regarding who comes through. Many cases of possession have been reported wherein a wayward energy eventually takes control of the body.

However, if you are really brave, look to some of the indigenous cultures for additional means of attaining higher consciousness. There are many ways this can be done from healing circles to sweat lodges to vision quests. Many South American and Indonesian medicine men attain a so-called trance consciousness by putting their physical body to sleep in order that their higher consciousness may be free to wander about unfettered by the earth-bound limitations of physical form. Native American shamans venture into other worlds to retrieve information or access the power of animal spirits.

Don't underestimate the value of a vision quest. Many young men from remote tribal societies seek their true nature by isolating themselves for months to become self-realized. Your author ventured out of his safe environment and went into the woods to spend three days alone. No food, no books, no Internet connection. On the third day, following an intense dialogue with a fuzzy caterpillar with which I bonded, I came out a changed person.

These are just a few ways, but find your own. You will know . . . you will feel it in your heart.

> Reality is nothing more than a collective hunch—Lily Tomlini

# 17

# The True Nature of Reality

Interestingly, the teaching of sages of Eastern Thought, many progressive sects of Christianity and the ancient and time-tested ways of the shamans are not entirely dissimilar. They all believe—to one degree or other—that dis-ease (illness) occurs from what they term as ignorance of the true nature of reality. Stated as an oversimplified concept, many from Tibetan spirituality to indigenous healers subscribe to the belief that sin and suffering occurs when the self or ego is thought to be separate from the Universal Spirit and it becomes the center of existence.

Rather than projecting their images of reality around their personality as we do in the West, many strive to perceive the Universe for what it truly is, peering through the illusion and attaining what might be called *the insight of emptiness* or the elimination of what is false. They have little need to submit to the intoxication of acquiring ever-increasing amounts of physical wealth. They have little fear of moving on to the next world when they drop the body in this one.

## East vs West

Conversely, we in the West, often correlate our almost fanatical worship of material wealth with our fear of dying—as if we are equally afraid of losing ourselves along with everything we have worked for when we drop our physical body. We tend to place a high priority on the external pleasures of life, such as money and power and often drift from one situation to another looking for satisfaction in external materialism. As a result, we often create false gods and images and give them our power and devotion.

The *Tibetan Book of the Dead*, a major work of the pre-Buddhist civilization of Tibet, suggests that one does not find truth from exterior materialism or even a guru or teacher, but finds it within. Shunryu Suzuki, a well-known Japanese Buddhist teacher said that, "taking refuge in physical possessions and transient pleasures merely deepens our confusion rather than ending it." [26] Even an old Tibetan adage suggests this concept when it states that if you are shot by an arrow, rather than being concerned as to who shot it and why, simply go about removing the arrow and treating the wound.

Maybe it is for this reason that many of the strict religious orders from a variety of spiritual philosophies require their students to reject all external possessions and take the vows of poverty. What this would imply is that when one refocuses on the inner work to the exclusion of the outer distractions, the real truth is discovered. The Eastern scholar advocates that when this inner peace is found, the outer world becomes secondary.

## Taking it to the next level

I believe the shaman and metaphysician take it to the next level by suggesting that once the real inner truth is known, the exterior world can be *manifested* to support what is truly believed to be true!

As Chamalu, an Andean shaman writes in his book, *The Gate of Paradise: Secrets of Andean Shamanism*, "Release the power that lies within you; you don't need to think a lot or remain a slave to reason. You are a being with power and this, you must never forget"

He goes on to state that Andean shamanism is the therapy of transformation and that the cure cannot be performed in this reality alone. He suggests that if you have not discovered the art of living, being fully who you are, then you are not completely awake. If your life does not flow naturally, sickness will knock on your door.

But isn't traveling this inner road really the way of most religions? Didn't both the Dalai Lama and Jesus tell us that *compassion* is the key word that leads us to our inner peace and a spiritual communion with the Divine Creator? Doesn't it make sense that if we each are individual portions of the compassionate Cosmic Whole, by simply letting go of judgments and cherishing ourselves as well as others we can find peace and harmony?

The Wesak Festival, the great Eastern festival of the Buddha, celebrates a sacred ceremony that takes place between the Buddha and the Christ as it pours a blessing upon our planet. It anticipates the time of change and expectancy while we await the World Teacher. Some call him the Christ; others the Maitreya, the Imam Mahdi, the Illuminati. All agree He is the source of light and love, inspiring and stimulating all efforts that foster human and planetary advancement.

## Universal consensus

In the meantime, wouldn't it be wonderful if we could somehow get Jesus, Buddha, Moses, Lao-tzu, and Zoroaster and a handful of avatars and "primitive" shamans together in the same room? I imagine there would be little difference on their viewpoints regarding the basic nature of reality? They would most likely agree that the mystical inner experience is the one true communion with what classical literature describes as the Godhead?

If this is true, maybe what we have been waiting and searching for has been there all along. Maybe the quiet faith and spiritual conviction of the downtrodden, such as the Tibetan people is, in truth, stronger than the vocal claims of those who profess their faith only to be distracted by the accomplishment-oriented, fast-paced world and then question their faith and commitment when the going gets tough.

Maybe the Tibetan people will survive after all.

## What is the lesson?

So ... what is the lesson here? During this author's extensive travels to sacred sites of the world, my wife and I searched for the hidden secrets and forgotten lessons of the true nature of reality. We visited the bowels of the ancient churches of Coptic Christianity, carved out of solid rock over 800 years ago in Ethiopia. We meditated in the King's Chamber of the Great Pyramid and were invited to meet mystics in ancient monasteries in the remote regions of Nepal, Tibet and Bhutan. We ingested ayahuasca with a shaman from a head hunting tribe in Ecuador and spent time in a ghost box, or manteum, in an attempt to meet deceased relatives with insight.

Did we attain the state of *savakalpa samadhi* that Dr. Mitchell spoke so highly about and encounter a higher recognition of reality and commune with the Divine?

I'm not sure that I really have a catchy phrase answer or a "one size fits all" philosophical riposte. We did not find a shortcut to meet God nor did we discover a well-marked roadmap to Nirvana. However, I can say with absolute certainty that our lives were changed by all we saw and experienced and we moved one step closer to understanding and living our own separate truths.

You might ask if the master plan is for us to find this so-called truth, why is it so well hidden and disguised?

For one thing, mankind has effectively destroyed the very secrets we seek to uncover. Sure, our modern technology has provided us the means to live longer and more comfortable lives. But in our passion to develop our science and expand our political influence, we have poisoned the environment that houses our outer or physical layer of being-ness. We have caused the extinction of thousands of species and are on pace to eliminate our protective ozone layer and our life-giving rain forests in just a few short decades. We have transformed less powerful societies to our political and spiritual way of thinking in order to self-perpetuate our belief system and way of life. The more people we can convert, the reasoning goes, the more secure we feel that we are right and all the others are misguided or lack understanding.

## Looking in the wrong place

Maybe in our search for easy to find spiritual certainty we are looking in the wrong places or at the wrong icons. Perhaps the inscrutable Sphinx and massive pyramids of Giza contain the answers as to who we really are. Maybe the giant monoliths of Stonehenge or the hidden city of Machu Picchu can provide the insight . . . if only we knew how to decipher their eerie silence. Perhaps the indigenous cultures that claim to receive their ancient wisdom from tea leaves, extraterrestrial aliens or forest elves have the answers.

No . . . I think Jesus, Buddha and all the other major spiritual avatars said it best when they suggested that the spiritual truths are where they always have been—inside each one of us. Mankind tends to partition the powerful Creator Force "up there somewhere" to fix things for us or to show us the way, rather than to search for the God consciousness within.

Like the Dorothy from Kansas when she landed in Oz—she went searching for the "all powerful wizard" before she discovered that she had the power all along. All she had to do was believe!

Since the Bible informs us that we are made in His image, maybe what it meant was that we are an aspect of this Creative Force, just as the beach is the sum total of all the individual grains of sand. And if this is so, it can be said that we are God experiencing His or Her Self.

And if that is true, we must possess the creative power to change what doesn't work.

Maybe we have had the answers all along . . .

And the key?

## The bottom line

I am sure there are many, just as there are many ways of living life, being creative or playing the game. But if you are on your spiritual search ... and are looking *inside* for the answers, then the key to getting there might be just to know that you can. And one of the tools to do this is the *intuitive* or *psychic knowing* that we all inherently have always possessed. All we have to do is to turn it on.

Shamans and mystics have developed this knowing in order to heal the sick, performing feats unexplainable by modern science. They have learned to harmonize their beingness with Mother Earth and listen to the wisdom of the ancestor spirits through their dreams.

I am here to tell you that you can do it too. You have the power.

And how do you do this? You just do it! You have been searching all your life and it has been available to you all this time.

Don't you just hate that?

> *You are the window through which you must see the world.* —Laura Ingalls Wilder

# 18

# Back to the Dream

Once we accept and understand that multiple levels of reality exist, all we need to do in order to access these abstract higher states of consciousness is—to know that it is possible. As we have discussed throughout the pages of this text, there exists a wide variety of means—all it takes is to look within . . . and believe.

This higher consciousness can be best attained while remaining safely grounded and connected with the earth plane. It is not necessary to shape shift as do the shamans, ingest psychedelic drugs in a hippie commune, travel out-of-body with a cave-dwelling guru or wait for a near death experience. What is necessary is to commit to the search and believe it is possible. Each person must find his or her own way, just as each artisan discovers his or her best method of expression.

The Creator's dream

It all comes back to the dream. Having been created in the image of the Dreaming Creator, we dream/imagine/affirm/manifest our life experience. This connection goes by many esoteric names such as prayer, meditation, past life recall, holotropic breathing and positive affirmations to mention just a few. Attaining this consciousness only requires a slight modification of your belief systems and a modest understanding of the nature of reality.

Since we have seen that we are the co-creators of our own individual dreams, script what best serves you. By conditioning your insight on "what is in my best interest," you will be better able to gain from the spiritual direction that follows.

Remember, you can always ask a guardian or spirit guide to assist you. By asking a question that begins with, "What do I need to know about—," you retain the power to do something about it. Prefacing your inquiry with demands to know "what is going to happen about . . . ." suggests that you are powerless to do anything about it. Remember, you control the future!

When asked how they go about doing this, some professional psychics and metaphysicians contend that when they seek direction from higher consciousness they "remember" the future as if it were a dream. Mystics and gurus are said to merely sit quietly and "know" the answer. Sounds like the same thing, doesn't it—just using different words to express a similar concept?

A shaman residing deep in the Amazon Rain forest of Ecuador summed it up this way: "Once we know what we want—all we have to do is *re-dream* it!"

## Let go of your limitations

I don't want to hear you say that you don't dream. If we are speaking of night dreaming while you sleep, I suggest that you dream, you just may not remember. Long ago, scientists proved that while they may not agree as to *why* we dream, we do it at least four to five times a night. They can tell you what the body does physiologically when it is dreaming, yet they still cannot agree on why.

Some in the medical profession have concluded that the only value of a dream is analyzing it in order to diagnose the ailment of their patient. Other highly educated professionals merely shrug dreams off as having little value other than possibly working off a few frustrations of life.

While the academic authoritarians prefer to remain caught up in their left-brain dialogue, why not simply assume responsibility for your life and cut to the chase? Dream the day dream, the higher spiritual dream. Move the cosmic, universal energy of which you are a part in the direction that best serves you.

Although the scientific community has provided many of the creature comforts of life we have grown to depend on, they tend to miss the point: the physical realm is *not* the only arena in which we can play. What if we don't color inside the lines or follow the rules they claim are the way things have to be? Once upon a time our experts said the universe revolved around our planet and the earth was flat. Not too long ago we accepted the notion that the horseless carriage was just a fad and that the telephone was an amusing toy that would never catch on.

Remember, these are the same experts in their field who were adamant that:

*"Heaver-than-air flying machines are impossible"*
Lord Kelvin, President Royal Society, nineteenth century

*"Everything that can be invented has been invented"*
Charles H, Duell, Director of U.S. Patent Office, 1899

# The Nature Of Reality...

*"Sensible and responsible women do not want to vote."*
Grover Cleveland, President of the United States, 1905

*"There is no likelihood man can ever tap the power of the atom."*
Robert Milikan, Nobel Laureate in Physics, 1923

*"Who the heck wants to hear actors talk?"*
Harry M. Warner, Warner Brothers Pictures, 1927

## Expand your awareness

When we let go of our limited view of what is possible we are able to access many levels of consciousness. Edgar Cayce went as far as to suggest that we actually can access the esoteric dimensions of the spirit world, if we believe we can. Cayce and others like him have claimed that there is *no limit* to what the human consciousness can access by using a few of the techniques suggested in these pages.

Is it even possible to communicate with other beings in other dimensions?

The ancient traditions of the Dogons from West Africa (located in what is now the Republic of Mali) speak of a "dark companion" of Sirius, the brightest star in the night sky from whence the seed of mankind came. It wasn't until modern technology provided telescopes that we were able to determine that Sirius did in fact have a faint binary companion star that rotated with Sirius around a common unseen point. How did they know that? Was its source a scientific text from their home based space travelers or communication from a great distance through the dream state?

## Dream the common dream

Since we all originated from the same original dream, anything is within the realm of possibility. Did you know our deeper conscious or dreaming mind is able to contact other dreamers awake or asleep? Try it yourself: gather a group of like-minded buddies, say on a camping trip, and agree before you go to sleep that you are going to share a common dream, and discuss the results the next morning around the camp fire. You will be surprised to discover a common theme emerging.

There are many ways we can become aware of information not otherwise perceived if we remain exclusively connected with the many daily physical distractions in our physical environment.

## Access your higher knowing

What you may not realize is that you have the ability and have accessed this higher knowing—you just may not have paid attention to the information. Think back to the last time you became alert to a situation when you somehow "knew" when something was wrong. Have you never known what was going to happen just before it occurred? Can you unequivocally state that you never had the feeling that you have been somewhere before when your logic says you haven't?

If you were to conclude that "knowing" something before it occurred was a random experience, I suggest it might have contained the fingerprints of your higher consciousness, guardian angel or spirit. What you might consider a coincidence, a spiritual master might label as a synchronistic event. Describe someone as lucky and I might offer the notion that the individual's expectation affected the outcome. What might be shrugged off as "feminine intuition" might be an awareness of knowing something on another level.

## Pay attention

Begin to pay attention to the daily clues around you—small stuff such as having a feeling that your friend would be late or that your team would not win. Some might suggest that you might have even caused the event to occur because you created a negative environment. Others might offer the notion that you were in touch with a higher awareness.

Both are probably right. The important thing is to know that you ultimately had a hand in creating your own personal experience.

Bottom line: You can do it. You are the co-producer and director of your own life dream. Don't give away your power. Take charge of your life and dream it the way you want it.

Show me where it says in your human owner's manual that it is *not* possible.

.

# REFERENCES

1. San Francisco Chronicle. October 19, 2000, David Perlman, science editor
2. San Francisco Chronicle, May 10, 2001, Davie Perlman, science editor.
3. Chapter CXIII, The Secret Teachings of All Ages, Manly Hall, The Philosophical Research Society, Inc, 1977
4. Stephanie Salter, San Francisco Chronicle page A21, April 17, 2002
5. 17th and 18th philosophy created by Christian Rosenkreuz
6. The alchemist followers of Hermes Trismegistus
7. William Morrow and Company, NY, NY 1995, pg 3
8. A character from a Dickens novel
9. Quartus Books, Austin Texas, 1984, page 44
10. The Power of Now, A guide to spiritual enlightenment, Eckhart Tolle, New World library, Novato. California 1999
11. Webster's New World Dictionary, Third College Edition, Prentice Hall, 1994
12. The Lost Teachings of Jesus, Mark and Elizabeth Prophet, Summet University Press, 986, Proligue li
13. Publisher John Wiley & Sons, 2001
14. Dr. Fred Wolf's book, The Dreaming Universe
15. The Lost Teachings of Jesus, page 32
16. The Book of Daniel
17. page 10, Visions and Prophecies, Time-Life Books, Alexandria, Virginia
18. Eck-vidya, Ancient Science of Prophecy, Paul Twitchell, Illuminated Way Publishing, Inc, Crystal, MN, 1982, page 63
19. Century 2, Quantrain 24 from The Centuries, a collection of

Nostradamus readings originally published under the name, The Prophecies of Michel Nostradamus

[20] For more information refer The Egyptian Heritage, published 1974 edited by Mark Lehner

[21] The Great Pyramid Decoded, Element Books, Ltd 1977

[22] Bob Thrift Institute for UFO Research, http:/www.frii.com

[23] The Occult, Barnes & Noble Books

[24] Time Magazine, Time Inc, NY April 10, 2000

[25] Yoga, Mind & Spirit: The Philosophy & Psychology of Yoga, Copyright 2001, Constance Habash

[26] Zen Mind, Beginners Mind, Weatherhill, 1982, pg 7

# About the Author

Chuck Coburn, psychic, teacher and TV host of Personal Pathways, stumbled on the doorway to these truths nearly 30 years ago when his life dramatically changed at precisely 6:45 PM on a Sunday evening in October 1979. He suddenly began to "know things" immediately following a three-day, self-awareness EST-like seminar. Within a few hours of completing this highly charged, emotional course, this practical, logic-based businessman began to experience dramatic and unexplainable psychic events.

Terrified, yet strangely intrigued by what was occurring, he began a frantic journey to seek answers to questions he wasn't even sure how to articulate. He desperately began his search to get a handle to what apparently was a latent ability he never knew he possessed.

This ability, he was to discover, is available to us all!

Obsessed with the need to understand this theosophical mid-life crisis, he found himself devouring numerous New Age books, submitting himself to uncomfortable touchy-feely workshops and listening to every self-proclaimed New Age guru who hit town. Eventually he was led to those whose guidance gently opened him further, from Western trained metaphysicians to numerous authentic indigenous shamans residing in various corners of the world; from the ayahuasca dispensing healer from a headhunting tribe in the Ecuadorian rainforest, to the current incarnation of the Karmapa, sequestered on the top of a sacred mountain in Tibet. He spent time with an African sandal thrower who talks to trees and with Ecuadorian healers who work with Orisha spirits and heal with eggs. He personally assisted a Brazilian psychic surgeon channeling the spirit of Dr Fritz and a healer who takes his direction from extraterrestrials.

As he wandered deeper into the dark woods of the unknown, a professional psychic, the grand niece of Albert Einstein, provided a structure for his undisciplined new energy. An interest in Mystic Christianity and ancient Buddhism led him to physical encounters with ghosts, spirit guides and "guardian angels." Further inquiries into spiritualism provided numerous communications with the energies of ghostly energies who have departed their bodies, all of which he chronicles in his previous two books.

He eventually closed down his successful construction business and became a professional psychic. He likes to say that he doesn't claim to channel Michael or Seth or bug-eyed green aliens from a galaxy beyond the unknown. Instead, he reportedly receives information and direction from his spirit guides – what he calls his personal advisors. Sami gives him the words, Joel keeps him focused and Amy, pumps him up when he needs direction. When asked to elaborate, he suggests that Amy is the spiritual energy that, in the words from the game of Monopoly, provides him the "get out of jail free" card when he needs the freedom but seldom allows him to "pass go and collect $200" when his ego gets out of check.

Get Published, Inc!
Thorofare, NJ 08086
19 August 2009
BA2009231